A Mind 4 Cricket

Raise your
game with
MENTAL
TRAINING

Paul Maher

Published by

MELROSE BOOKS

An Imprint of Melrose Press Limited
St Thomas Place, Ely
Cambridgeshire
CB7 4GG, UK
www.melrosebooks.com

FIRST EDITION

Copyright © Paul Maher 2011

The Author asserts his moral right to
be identified as the author of this work

Cover designed by Jeremy Kay

ISBN 978 1 907040 82 5

Printed and bound in Great Britain by:
CPI Antony Rowe. Chippenham, Wiltshire

MIX
Paper from
responsible sources
FSC® C013604

This copy of *A Mind 4 Cricket* you have purchased is for your own personal use. You are welcome to copy to CD-ROM or other storage media for backup for your own personal use.

Membership to the website www.mindtrainingarena.com entitles you to any future messages, updates and bonus reports. Electronic books, known as e-books are protected worldwide under international copyright and intellectual property law, the same as printed books, recorded material and other literary works.

FOREWORD

The information contained in this book is intended for people in good health. The ideas, suggestions and techniques are not a substitute for proper medical advice. Anyone with medical problems of any kind should consult a medical practitioner. The author does not prescribe any techniques described here as a form of treatment for any physical or mental problems. Any application of the ideas, suggestions or techniques is at the reader's sole discretion.

This publication contains the author's opinion on the subject matter covered herein. The intent of the author is to offer information to help you in your effort to improve your cricket, so there is no warranty of any kind for any particular purpose. If you use any of the information in this publication for yourself or others, neither the author nor publisher is liable or responsible to any person or entity for any consequential, incidental or special damage caused or alleged to be caused directly or indirectly by the information contained within.

CONTENTS

PREFACE

A Mind 4 Cricket was originally written for players of all levels as a practical guide to help them get the maximum benefit from their cricket, so they can perform consistently with excellence. My research found next to nothing on the bookshelves on mental skills training for cricket, and since receiving favourable comments on and interest in what is a motivating, thought-provoking and performance-changing book, this updated and expanded volume is intended to answer some of the questions I have been asked since the original 2008 publication.

More knowledge within the cricket community on the mind in sports performance has come from the large amount of research undertaken in recent years, especially from Australia. Most professional cricketers, followed by an increasing number of recreational players, now better understand how to improve their confidence, belief and motivation and master their emotions. However, I have yet to meet any one cricketer who fully appreciates all of his/her strengths and weaknesses. Everyone has attitudes, behaviour, inclinations and preferences of which they are not fully aware.

My purpose is to teach you how to change the way you think and give you tools so you can achieve your goals and reach your full potential, if that is what you truly desire. Although only one player each season can become Player of the Year, this book can help you become the heart and soul of your team. The techniques here come from sport psychology, neuro-linguistic programming (NLP), along with ideas from my own experience in sport hypnosis.

NLP, referred to as the 'science of success', is steadily becoming recognised for its tools that benefit a sportsperson in reaching quick and lasting changes and a positive mindset. By the time you have read this book, you will know some powerful methods which create positive change in your game, or that of those you coach.

The term 'sport psychologist', as understood by most people in sport, may intimidate some cricketers. Traditions go back a long way, so new ideas are often frowned upon. Twenty years ago, acupuncture was laughed at in the west, but it is now a fully accepted therapy.

I feel that the more recent titles 'mental skills coach' or 'perform-ance enhancement coach' are far more appropriate and will be accepted more easily by cricketers as indicating somebody who is trained to guide them to use the resources of their mind more effec-tively and gain a positive, winning attitude.

When you become successful, you will feel good about yourself, what you do and what you have. Then your life becomes a better place to be.

Enjoy your cricket.

Paul Maher MA

INTRODUCTION

Our fascination with cricket is that it never ceases to fascinate.

David Rayvern Allen

Welcome. I want to share with you techniques that will motivate you to succeed in your cricket, teach you strategies that have helped many cricketers break through their limitations, and control your thinking, so you can play the game others dream of. Throw away any limitations forever, the quality of your game will catapult you to new heights – after all, the achievements of one player can energise and inspire their whole team.

Cricket is a great game, providing opportunities to grow and evolve. Remember as a child the excitement of unwrapping your first cricket bat? It won't take long to read this manual, but the techniques you learn will serve you in your career and beyond. Your playing career can be over before you know it; you owe it to yourself to have a stormer.

Let me answer that question going on in your mind… what's it all about? Mental skills and sport psychology are not modern concepts, they've been around for as long as sports have been played and are as much about mental attitude as solid technique. It now plays an increasing role in shaping a player's performance.

Clinical sport psychology will assist a cricketer to conquer or remove a variety of mental symptoms and challenges they would normally struggle with, and help to expand the psychological and behavioural qualities which will also improve the cricketer's physical capabilities for improved sporting performance.

It must be stressed that sport psychology, as well as hypnosis, cannot make a person without talent become a top-class player, but they will considerably help those with talent to develop better performance.

NLP was developed in the mid-seventies by John Grindler, a university lecturer in linguistics, and Richard Bandler, a computer programmer, as a way to identify how people regulate their behaviours subconsciously and, if required, re-programme their minds. Handy techniques taught here will guide you toward these powerful, positive changes. Your mind is the most important body part you can train; here I'll show you how to reach your full potential.

Your mind consists of both your conscious mind – you are using it now as you are aware of sitting there reading this book – plus your subconscious mind, also known as the unconscious mind. That is a huge understatement as it is not unconscious, it is not asleep – you could say it is super-conscious.

As a human, you have an incredible mind that can sometimes get wired up in a way that is not useful for some situations you find yourself in. The subconscious mind acts in a literal, even naïve way. As it's non-judgemental, it will absorb a bad idea as much as a good one. Culture, family, peer pressure, a bad coach, all teach ways that mentally just aren't useful for what you want to achieve.

If you're cynical, believe learning is boring, think this is all weird new-age stuff, we need to have a chat. It does work. Hundreds of therapists like myself and thousands of clients say it does work. There are poor therapists about, so if you or a colleague have tried something like this before and failed, get over it! Sorry to be so blunt, but doom-mongers and nay-sayers will never become better cricketers.

This book is just like having me sit down with you and go over, step-by-step, exactly how to do the techniques. The goal is to help you get greater control of yourself and cricket by planting positive suggestions in your mind. The secret to successful cricket is very simple. Do something… anything at all! Even if you mess up you will be wiser for the experience. You have to take action, that is what separates winners from losers.

Read this book from cover to cover and then read it again. Make it an ongoing journey. The more you can digest this information, the more it will have an impact on your cricket. All of these techniques need to be practised; find ten minutes every day to work on the ones you find interesting.

Use this book as an interactive tool to challenge, excite, inspire and teach. Don't underestimate the methods, you can find them invaluable. If you consider a technique strange or not to your liking, simply find another that you can adjust to suit your need – there will be a more exciting one for you on another page.

Allow yourself some quiet space and time to go through these techniques properly. It can all start with one technique and it will start by knowing that technique well. Don't attempt to go all out to learn them all right away. Learn one then extend your range. Even the simple act of doing a minor one can get you moving on to others.

I have made examples of situations you may find yourself in, but you're free to use them as a template which can be changed and adapted to suit your needs. They are not quick-fix miracle cures, you have to put the time in to learn and use them, but the successful methods you are about to learn will help you begin making a wave of changes, now, on this first day. Chances are you will be bitten by the bug as you find your confidence grow. Excited? You should be. These methods can rock you to your core. These methods can also affect other areas of your life.

Get padded up, it all starts here...

FOR COACHES

Mental preparation in cricket is perhaps 90% to 99% of importance to overall game preparation.

Jonathan Batty

Getting the best from your players is one of the greatest skills required by any coach. How well you communicate depends on your players' response, which means you are responsible for how they understand you. Pay attention to the words you use as your words can open up the possibility for positive change in your team members. There is a chapter later on about using words which you may find revealing.

Mental skills training is something you do WITH a player, not TO a player. If you are using the methods in this book on any of your players, there are a number of steps to take for best results:

○ Explain the process to your player or players.

○ Establish where the player or players are with a particular mental attitude and where they, or you, would like them to be. This is best provided by using a benchmark of zero to ten, with zero being nothing, no problem at all, and ten being very problematic. Take anxiety, for example, with a young spin bowler about to make his first team appearance: zero will be very calm and prepared, while ten will be extremely anxious.

1

○ Use one of the techniques, then apply the zero to ten bench-mark scale again to find if your young player's anxiety has reduced.

○ Before attempting a technique, you must know if it is absolutely right to correct your players' thinking. Are there any negative consequences? You must be sure there will only be good, ethical consequences to come from making any change to their mindset. This is best by asking these useful questions:

    ○ *What is the purpose of this change?*

    ○ *What will the player gain or lose by it?*

    ○ *What will happen if they make the change?*

    ○ *What will not happen if the player does not make the change?*

○ Perform the technique.

○ Check the technique has worked and your player has shown an improvement. Remember the zero to ten scale.

○ Next, ask your player to imagine a future situation which previously would have created their issue and notice how they now feel about it. Repeat this as often as you feel is necessary until your player is convinced their attitude has changed for the better. Pay attention to any non-verbal communication your player is showing. Is their voice tone and body language in accord with their verbal responses?

Be aware that some, though very few, players may have repressed or traumatic memories which are beyond your ability to change and may be best dealt with by a qualified therapist. Some NLP techniques are surprisingly powerful and can have a greater impact on your player than you may realise. Is there a history of mental illness or depression? Are they on medication? Do they have a history of epilepsy? If in doubt, DO NOT work with them.

Often coaches will tell a player when something is wrong, then give misleading advice on how to correct it by inventing all kinds of theories. Even comments like 'you should do better' can place the player on a long, lonely road. Please do not coach natural ability out of young players. Encourage their strengths without getting too technical and theoretical. Allow a young batsman to play his strokes if they produce runs; that's what counts, not textbook form.

At the heart of the mastery of coaching are the personal qualities of leadership, confidence, knowledge and self-reliance. Competent coaches have a great influence on the lives of their players. They are masters at communication and building team spirit. Good coaches care. They support their players, especially if a player is suffering from some form of setback or injury. They challenge their players to grow and become the best they can be in a positive and respectful manner.

In contrast, various elements can lead to conflict which will be marked by lack of interest from the player, a lack of commitment, remoteness, even deceit, antagonism and abuse. Misunderstandings will frequently develop. Good communication promotes appreciation, commitment, dependence, trust, respect, and will go far in developing knowledge and understanding about cricket issues.

A performance enhancement coach (PEC) can evaluate your players' general character, including the ways they learn, solve problems and deal with pressure. Nobody manages pressure as much as they think they do. We all become frustrated and irritable with things we are acquainted with, and there are also things we may not be aware of that cause us stress. A good PEC can help with external and internal stressors and teach techniques to minimise or eliminate any negative emotions.

Cricketers can also be influenced by a PEC who is trained in valuable hypnotic interventions as these methods can enable positive change for a cricketer who needs quick results to achieve potential, have a better attitude, maintain motivation and give greater discipline to training behaviour.

Do you understand yourself…?

WHAT ABOUT YOU?

Be yourself, everyone else is already taken.

Oscar Wilde

You're surrounded. Almost all the fielders are within touching distance. You take your guard, get your feet right, your grip. With maybe eight fielders around the bat there's no sport quite as intense as cricket. You look around. Eleven against YOU! Are you bold enough to stand up to them?

Your forthcoming behaviour is a result of your self-image, the person you believe you really are. Your self-image is so strong your behaviour will have you perform consistently as that person you think you are.

We all know people who are skilled, yet think they are not. They believe they are too fat, too slow, too old, too out of shape, whatever. If you believe that about yourself, if you believe yourself not good enough in any way, you will subconsciously sabotage any effort to make yourself a winner. Batting too defensively only creates confidence in the bowler.

Studies have proven time after time that an extraordinary number of sportspeople fail because they think themselves less than they are worth through this limited self-image. Are they unworthy? Of course

y see themselves in their imagination which affects
ce and can even cause self-destructive behaviour.

example to prove my point. Sit for a moment some-
ad remember some time in the past when you felt tired,
sad, despondent. Really get back into that time by remembering
everything you could see and hear in as much detail as you can. Bring
back any physical and emotional experiences, get that memory and
hold it for a few seconds. Try to stand up.

Now sit down again and this time bring back to mind a time
when you felt energetic, determined, optimistic. Again remember in
as much vivid detail as you can what you saw, hear the good things
you heard and get in touch with the physical and emotional feelings
you had and hold them for several seconds. Now stand up.

Compare the two experiences. In the first you may have found
it an effort to stand. How about the second? Did you leap up, ready
to go? Notice that your thoughts influence how you perform. Isn't it
interesting that in just a few seconds, thinking one way then another
created an entirely different result? Your belief about yourself influences your thoughts which then affect your behaviour, as this book
will prove.

That said, let me remind you how quickly your cricketing
career goes by. For instance, it's incredible how the last twelve
months have gone by. How was it? Think about your mortality.
Imagine you're breathing your last. Did you do all you wanted to do
in cricket? Did you truly live it? Visit the venues you always wanted
to? Enjoy wonderful moments with your team-mates? Before you
know it, you find yourself retired, then into old age and there you
are, staring into emptiness, reflecting on how good you could have

been. That's how it ends up for the vast majority of people. Where did all the time go?

The only thing you have total control of in this world is your thinking. At first you may feel self-conscious trying out these methods. Whenever you do something new which takes you beyond your comfort zone you feel nervous. It's OK, you're human. You must grit your teeth and get out of your comfort zone. Good mental preparation before is then as good as physical preparation.

So, do you have a good in-depth understanding of yourself? Do you recognise and value your temperament and character? Do you know the benefits as well as any risk associated with your own style of game? Beware, people often see what they want to see when it comes to self-evaluation. Solid self-understanding will certainly influence your cricket career.

Calm individuals are not as affected emotionally by success and failure as excitable people. Calm makes it easier to concentrate – however, being more laid-back may make someone slower to react to certain conditions.

Excitable individuals are almost always on the go and are at risk of reacting too quickly emotionally. These people also use up a lot of time and valuable energy being so intense.

Ask three or four friends or team-mates, people you can trust, to grade their impressions of you. What would they say your internal mental strengths are? Your best psychological ability? Include attributes of attitude, competitiveness, confidence, versatility. Spend some time reflecting on what they said. Do you agree?

This book will open up to you clear ideas as to what you need to do to create the cricket future you want. Nothing in your life is going to change unless you change. You are fully capable of mental and physical feats. You are bigger than you think, capable of more than you can imagine.

Let's move on to how your mind functions…

YOUR MIND

Minds are like parachutes, they only work when they are open.

Marc Salem

By understanding how your mind functions, you will be able to utilise its power to get the most from yourself or those you coach. It is often claimed we use less than ten percent of our mind, so its vast, latent power is still unknown to medical research.

Your mind has two parts, the conscious and the subconscious, otherwise known as the unconscious. Some spiritual people also believe we have a super-conscious. Your conscious mind functions in a state of active awareness. So as you are reading this book, you are aware of the words on the page. Your conscious mind thinks and plans. You consciously set targets and goals, plan tactics, decide what skills to practise. For example, during a game you may decide to bowl a fast spin around the wicket after bowling over the wicket to change the angle of delivery and confuse the batsman.

Your subconscious however has much more depth to it, in fact the depth is immeasurable. Are you aware of your breathing? Of your digestion? When you sleep, who does those functions for you? Your subconscious. It runs your body, contains all you memories, holds

9

your values and your emotions. Using the bowling example above, having consciously decided what to bowl, your subconscious takes over to co-ordinate your physical movements, so you use the necessary skill gained from constant practice without any conscious mind interference.

The batsman receiving your ball will be unlikely to react consciously with any judgement as he has no idea where you are bowling and the ball could be travelling and swerving at ninety miles per hour, so he will have to act instinctively.

That's why you practise. Your subconscious mind will find it difficult to perform a task it has never seen or executed. The better you practise, with constant repetition, the more automatic, competent and smooth your actions become. When it is not possible to physically practise, you can visualise by using your imagination.

Your subconscious responds to symbolic thought. It sees, hears, feels, smells and tastes. So imagine standing at the crease; you will see the ball in your mind's eye, hear the sound as you hit it, physically feel the connection of your bat and perhaps smell the freshly mown outfield.

Your conscious and subconscious minds can best be described like this. Your conscious mind is the team captain, planning tactics, setting targets, analysing the opposition. It's the task of the team, your subconscious mind, to follow the captain's instructions and make his plans happen on the field.

While there is good communication between the captain (your conscious mind) and the team (your subconscious mind) and the team are well drilled in their duties from training and practice, all should play efficiently. If there is poor communication brought about by low confidence, negative thought, indecision, poor skills, then you can imagine what the performance on the field will be like.

Returning to our bowling example, you decide what you are going to bowl, then at the last second you change your mind during your run up; you then impede your body's natural flow, creating poor communication between captain and team, poor communication between conscious and subconscious minds.

That is why practice is so important, especially working on new techniques or improving specific skills. The more you practise them, the more automatic they become for you and you are better able to reproduce them without having to stop and think during a match. Please remember, perfect practice makes perfect performance.

Your subconscious is like a loyal servant, it wants to please you. However, it only has the ability to do so through simple communication. As you have learnt, your subconscious is huge, but it needs direction. It responds best through your senses rather than words, which is great for skills practice.

Say it more with words...

IT'S ONLY WORDS

I think I had about eight names for the one that went straight.

Shane Warne

Master the words you use and you get more results from your life. Your subconscious thinks in images and symbols, so you need to structure the language you use to create images in your mind about what good things you want to happen or what you desire. Pay particular attention to your thoughts and the words you use as twenty percent of them have strong emotional undertones, having either a positive or negative effect on you.

In her book, *Every Word Has Power*, Yvone Oswald tells us the overall impact of productive, high-energy words such as *better*, *fine*, *good*, *great*, *healthy*, *welcome* and *wealth* is that they resonate at a higher frequency and give you a better quality emotion than limiting, low-energy words like *difficult*, *hard*, *nasty* or *problem*.

You can begin to realise how much more positively you speak when the low-energy words are no longer used, as the high-energy words become more liberating.

Words you must be careful about using consist of the following:

But. Using *but* implies judgement. It also cancels out any sentence used before it. So, if your coach says, 'You played well today, but you bowled too many no-balls,' the coach need not have said anything. 'You played well today and perhaps you can avoid no-balls' is more encouraging. Also *but* is often followed by an excuse for not doing something. 'I wanted to train, but…' If you replace *but* with *and* it gives a far better perspective.

Can't. Don't. Not. Your subconscious does not understand a negative. *Don't think about your team captain.* What did you think? Did your captain come into your mind? *Don't think of an umpire with green hair.* What happened? Your subconscious responds to the key words you give it, so has difficulty processing a negative. The subconscious mind has the maturity of a seven-year-old. Tell a seven-year-old not to touch something and see what happens.

Which is the better sentence:

Don't take your eye off the ball.

Keep your eye on the ball.

The first sentence has you thinking about what you don't want to be happening, while the second has you knowing what to do. For coaches, do your best to avoid telling a player what you *don't* want.

Two more words to lose from your vocabulary are *try* and *hope* for the confusion they create in your subconscious. You either do, or you do not, do something. When you *try* or *hope* you are telling yourself it's going to be difficult and setting yourself up for failure. Here's why. If I ask you to try to pick up a bat lying at your feet and you do, you have failed. Why? Because I did not ask you to pick up the bat, I asked you to try. Have you ever felt uncertainty when someone asks you to try to do something? Now you know where the uncertainty comes from.

Read these two sentences:

I will try to improve my fielding.

I will improve my fielding.

Of the two sentences, the second resonates with the intention to improve and sounds more convincing. Put it like this, plants don't try to grow, they grow. Birds don't try to fly, they fly. Do you try to pay your club's fees, or do you pay them?

When you hope for something, your subconscious automatically puts it into the unreachable section of your mind.

How about changing *why* to *how* or *because*.

Use *when* instead of *if*.

Should or *must* give people a feeling of guilt when they 'should do' or 'must do' but don't. 'I should/must concentrate when fielding.' 'I should/must practise leg spin.' How does that make you feel in your body? Turn them into *want* so they become 'I want to concentrate when fielding'; 'I want to practise leg spin'. Is that *want* feeling different from *should* and *must*? Does it make you more determined? Does it give you a desire to achieve? 'Want' power can be as good as 'will' power.

Whenever you realise you have made a negative statement, restate what you said as a positive statement by beginning the sentence with 'in the past'. So 'I'm always lbw against left-armers' can now become 'In the past I used to be lbw by left-armers'.

As I'm sure you now realise, there are never any 'problems' when you reframe them as 'challenges' or 'opportunities'.

You're in the process of thinking with belief...

BELIEF

Man is what he believes.

Anton Chekhov

You're the opening batsman. You need concentration, discipline, courage and self-control to blunt the onslaught of an aggressive fast bowler looking for blood. There's a new ball and you may face a close, attacking field. As an opener you must be switched on or your game is in trouble. Belief gives you the assurance to stamp your will on the game.

Belief dominates behaviour whether positively or negatively and behaviour affects performance. Your physical behaviour is controlled by belief. A belief is knowing with absolute certainty what something means. That belief can mean the difference between an ordinary player and a world conqueror. Success or failure. You always prove yourself right. However, a lower order batsman with a good technique can improve with the desire belief can bring.

Whether you believe you can do something, or believe you can't, you're right!

In other ways belief can determine your quality of happiness, health, wealth and success. It even has a greater influence on your life than the actual truth.

16

Notice the successful players. They have made more mistakes than those who aren't successful. Every mistake has been used as a learning opportunity for them. They continued to believe in themselves. Failure is part of the learning process, not the end of it. Don't be afraid to fail successfully, it's only a frustration.

When have you failed? Only when you stopped believing. Every response was information to tell you what actions were getting you closer to or further away from what you wanted.

We all get stuck in our beliefs, however sensible we think they are. You may find it interesting that you tend to believe what you think is true, without question. If you believe you can't spin bowl, it's because you believe you can't spin bowl. But the interesting thing is, if you tell yourself you can, that then gives you permission to question that defeatist belief and soon, with consistent practice, you will find that you can spin bowl – can't you! What you believe isn't necessarily real, you just have to invest in yourself. Confused? The nice thing about being confused is you come out of it with something new.

Do this. Get a piece of paper and write 'I can't' about ten times. Then go back to the top and finish each sentence with something that applies to cricket such as:

I can't spin bowl

I can't keep my eye on the ball

Seriously challenge yourself if each sentence is something you really cannot do, so extend the sentence to include something like 'but I will learn'. Or is it a skill you have not developed? If so, end the sentence with 'I would like to improve on this'.

Whether you believe you can do something, or believe you can't, you're right!

Mental blocks are often difficult to deal with as they involve you changing your belief regarding what you can or cannot do. Usually when there is a mental block, there could be something happening in your personal life affecting how you see a mixture of concerns. If you're bottling up any feelings regarding cricket, you may well begin to see the downside of what you can or cannot achieve. These negative beliefs then surface as mental blocks, losing self-confidence for you and increasing frustration or anxiety.

Belief creates self-talk, how you speak to yourself inside your head. If you're going to say something to yourself, you may as well make it something good.

Whether you believe you can do something, or believe you can't, you're right!

Take a belief which is holding you back.

Think about or write down its opposite, more positive belief.

Imagine what it would be like living this new belief.

Believe that:

You do have the ability to succeed.

You can accomplish anything.

There are no problems, just opportunities.

You're creating your future now.

If you begin to believe you're destined to be a successful cricketer, you will be.

As you can gather, just because you believe something, it doesn't necessarily mean it's true. You can reconsider your beliefs and decide which are useful to yourself and should be maintained, and those negative beliefs which you now know can be changed. A beneficial belief-change you can make here and now is that you can master the techniques in this book, very easily and quickly.

Now, that kind of thinking can give you a buzz you won't believe!

And the openers? Some openers bide their time, playing the patience game, gauging the behaviour of the pitch, the pace of the bowlers, going onto the back foot and taking low-risk shots. However, some will believe the ball is there to be hit, asserting the authority of their strokes from the start. That's where their mental side comes in, confident in the face of the bowler's hostility.

Whether you believe you can do something, or believe you can't, you're right! Am I getting the point across?

Believe in the power of your imagination...

IMAGINATION

You can't build a reputation on what you're going to do.
It's simple; fantasize, rehearse, then go out into the world
and do it!

Henry Ford

Imagine that I have just cut a lemon in two and I've handed you one of the halves. Notice its texture there in your hand as you bring it up to your mouth. Be aware of the citric smell while you place the juicy fruit in your mouth. Now suck on all that tangy lemon juice and let it run down your throat.

As you're reading this, imagine both of your hands are submerged in a bucket of hot, soapy water. You can remember what that's like? Did you have a bath last night? Wash the windows? Even your car? Recall that feeling of hot soapy water on your hands, make it vivid, feel those pinpricks of watery heat.

Your subconscious mind can't tell the difference between a real or imagined event, it's just like a VCR. It records sights and sounds continuously. Your body then treats every vivid thought and image as if it was real. Ever awakened from a nightmare? Notice how your body responds to the vivid use of your imagination more than to a conscious command. If you order your heart to speed up, it probably won't. If you imagine in detail walking down a dark sinister alley late at night and hear fast approaching footsteps behind you, I bet your heartbeat will increase. What about that nightmare? It wasn't real but you woke up in a sweat, your heart pounding, gripped with fear, and it took a while for you to calm down.

Everyone has the ability to imagine, I may have just proven it to you. If not, answer these questions:

Think of your locker in the changing room. What does it look like? Where is the door handle? What sound does it make when you shut it?

To answer you had to use your imagination. Now by changing the pictures and sounds in your mind, you can gain conscious control of any aspect of your game. Images that are bigger, brighter, bolder have a greater impact than those which are smaller, duller and further away. Let me show you.

Think of someone you found stressful to play against or who rankled you. Think about facing them again. A bad memory can hurt you like a knife. They can beat you without a ball being bowled. Here's something you're going to love. Recall their face. As you do so, ask yourself:

Is the memory in colour or black and white?

Is their face in your memory to the left, to the right, or there, right in front of you?

Is it large or small?

Is it light or dark?

Moving or still?

21

Are there any sounds?

Now play around with the way you are remembering that person. Make each of these changes in turn and notice what happens:

If the memory has colour, drain it all away until it is like a black and white photo.

Move the position of the image and push it further away from you.

Shrink it down in size.

Turn down the brightness, make it fuzzy.

If the image is moving, freeze-frame it.

What sound do you hear? Is it their voice? Change it by giving them a squeaky voice like a cartoon character, or a deep sexy one – go on, do it.

Finally, give the face a clown's nose, bright orange or green hair, Mickey Mouse ears. Go on, have fun!

Altering your memory can change how you feel. Think of the person again in this new way. How do you feel? Probably the stressful memory has diminished, if not gone completely. Not only do you feel different now, imagine how comfortable you will feel the next time you face that person. It's your control, your emotions, your thinking that belongs to you, not someone controlling you.

Let me show you how to use imagination in a way known as *association and dissociation* (there will be a detailed chapter on this next). Think of another stressful or uncomfortable memory. Keep that image in your mind, now step out of yourself so you can see the back of your head. (I know you may be sceptical, at least give me a hearing.) Now move away as far from the situation as you can. Step all the way out of the picture so you can still see it, but way over there somewhere as if it's happening to someone else. Shrink it down. Lose all the colour. Turn the background fuzzy or white. Fade away any sound. Notice that dissociation reduces the intensity of the feelings you were having. It takes courage to learn new skills such as these.

You can do the same to heighten a good memory with association. When you think about happy memories, you recreate the happy feelings associated with them. Remember a time when you felt really confident, aware of your ability, strength and self-belief. Now let the image come into your mind, make it juicy. Step into that memory as if you're there again, seeing through your own eyes, hearing through your ears and feeling how successful you felt in your body. Enlarge the memory, make it bigger and brighter, the feelings stronger, turn up the sounds and make them richer. If you can't remember a time, imagine how it would feel to be totally confident. You get what you focus on.

That's it! To reduce a negative memory, step out, move away from it (dissociate). Watch it as if it's happening to someone else, shrink it, turn it black and white, dull, out of focus. Make the sounds quieter, further away. Doing this can cause any bad emotional response to drain away. Notice that you're controlling how it affects you.

To improve a positive memory, zoom in and fully experience it (associate). Make the image bigger and closer, intensify the colour, increase the brightness, make the sounds closer, louder, unless it's a memory of peace and quiet. Live it. You can have a great deal of fun with these methods.

Imagine you're batting. Step into a picture of yourself controlling the ball, hitting fours and sixes almost at will. Feel mighty and proud. Hear the 'thunk' of every perfectly hit ball. Notice the fielders. Slip catchers, a gully, a short leg. Shrink them down and turn them into black and white, move them further away from you, duller, quieter. The bowler unable to penetrate or establish any rhythm…

Now go through the same process, but as a bowler – go on, I'm not going to do everything for you!

Visualise winning a trophy and holding it up. Feel its weight, the touch of cold metal. See from your mind's eye, out. See from the supporters' perspective. From the club officials' view. Picture yourself on the field holding the trophy from different angles. A champion wins in the mind first.

You can use your imagination to free yourself of any old, negative beliefs that might be limiting you. That's right! Imagine them written or painted on a wall. Gripping a bat in your hands, attack the wall, demolish it completely, see the dust, hear the noise of bricks tumbling, feel the energy you're using until the words or images are totally destroyed.

You could imagine them drawn or written on paper. Feel the paper between your hands as you rip it to shreds, hear it, feel it, see it happen there in your mind's eye. Finish off by ritually burning it. I said some methods would challenge you – this is all revolutionary stuff!

Here's an easier one. Close your eyes and imagine in your mind a picture of the player you wish to become. See how you will be dressed, your balanced stance, the expression on your face, all the tiny details. Take that picture and throw it up into the air and multiply it so that hundreds of copies come raining down all around you as far as your eye can see. They even go into your past and your future.

Did that feel awkward? Exercises like these may seem silly, but while you control the pictures in your mind and how they sound, you're not at the mercy of anyone else or of circumstances, and they direct your subconscious mind toward being the cricketer you want to be. A flame will ignite inside you.

Maybe imagine once or twice not doing as well, so that you can bring your emotions into it. Don't just visualise the best-case scenarios. Be prepared with a plan B and also a plan C. Don't imagine failing, but mentally plan how you will respond to unpleasant or difficult situations. This happens sooner or later when games do not go exactly as you hoped. You can still be proud of putting one hundred percent effort in.

Over to association and dissociation…

ASSOCIATION & DISSOCIATION

When I step across the boundary rope, that is the only time I feel I am in total control.

Dickie Bird

Here is where your imagination or visualisation skills pay off, as when you remember or mentally rehearse, you do it through association or dissociation.

Association, as you have learnt, means reliving an event as if it is really happening to you, seeing through your own eyes, hearing the sounds through your own ears and feeling all the feelings, whereas dissociation is noticing the situation as if you are watching yourself in a movie. As you are more detached from the situation, there is less emotional impact, as that is where you want to be if it is a problematic event.

Which of these two exercises feels more natural for you?

Think of a time when you had a bad game. How did you feel? As you remember it, are you looking at it through your own eyes or are you watching yourself as if in a movie? How about a great game? How are you seeing it? How are you feeling about it?

Recall the bad game. If you are associated, seeing through your own eyes, step away from it so you are watching yourself in a film. Do your emotions feel less? If you happen to feel worse when you dissociate, re-associate into it. If you are okay with the dissociation, keep it at that as there is no need to associate into a bad memory.

Now go back to that great game you played. Are you associated or dissociated? If you are associated, notice how dissociating lessens the way you feel. Likewise, if you are dissociated, notice the impact when you associate in.

You can also use association and dissociation for mental rehearsal. Think of an important game coming up, a cup game perhaps. Imagine watching yourself play so you are dissociated. There are some aspects you should be aware of. Remember the person (you) is hearing things going on around the ground as well as inside that person's head. Besides noticing how their body moves, be aware of any emotions that may be going on inside their body.

Spend some time on this exercise and look at 'you' from all perspectives, front, side, back and above.

Then repeat the exercise by associating into it. Be there inside your body as if it is really happening. See everything you would see, hear all the sounds including the positive words you would say to yourself. Feel everything both physically and emotionally.

How was that?

Imagine this. Whenever you're batting and approaching the nervous nineties, you are attacked by nerves. Your thoughts become distractions, you back off and take your eye off the ball. Psychologically it's becoming an issue for you as you keep rerunning missed opportunities in your mind. Here's a visualisation you can have a go at. Players in other positions can adapt this for themselves.

First, remember or visualise yourself sitting in the pavilion (associated) during a game, watching yourself in the middle getting closer to your century (dissociated). What encouragement and advice would you give to that 'you' who is batting? Let that mental film run while you watch yourself and stop at the point where you are usually bowled or caught. Being dissociated, this should help you remember the moment without the negative emotional content.

Freeze-frame that image. Here's where you get to have fun. Play with the image. If it is in colour, turn it black and white. If its clear, de-focus. Is it bright? If so, make it dim. Is it in a frame or not? Change any sounds, make them quieter. Change the location of any noises. Change any feelings.

Rewind. Start the film again in all its glory; this time associate into it so you are there, playing, and speed everything up until you reach the point just before you are out. Now, play the film at normal speed and adjust everything you like which will turn the ending into a hook or a sweep as you continue to send the ball flying toward the boundary.

Celebrate your success, feel how good you will feel scoring your century, feel the pride. Dissociate now and go back to the pavilion so you are associated and applaud yourself. Give positive, useful feedback. Repeat that visualisation several times a day until it feels like real memory.

Remember, for most people, dissociating from the memory of a bad event reduces any emotion, which gives it less power, while associating into a positive scenario brings in pleasant memories and emotions.

It will boost your confidence…

CONFIDENCE

The only thing I am frightened of is getting out.

Geoff Boycott

Making a big catch or finishing the season with a trophy can give you a huge boost. The one big key toward cricket success, however, is confidence, as the more confident you are, the more effective your performance will be.

Confidence makes you look like you mean business. It is the intent you are giving out so it is important to distinguish between confidence in yourself as a person, dependability toward commitments, integrity, honesty, sincerity, your values and the various roles you play in your life, plus your performance confidence, being one of those roles.

Let's look at how you can develop more performance confidence. On a piece of paper, make two columns where you are going to write down all your essential elements that are relevant to cricket. Make a heading on the first column, 'practical skills', as this is where you put your bowling delivery, batting, fitness, and in the second column put 'interpersonal skills' as here you will list things like assertiveness, communication, confidence, resilience.

Come back to this list on a regular basis as new thoughts come to you. Get some feedback from your coach, team-mates, friends, those whose opinion you can trust. Write down everything no matter how insignificant you may at first think, especially in column two as there you will find an indirect but noteworthy influence on your career.

When the list is finally complete, rate yourself out of ten on each aspect you have written down. Be honest. Resist the urge to rate yourself as much as you would like. Show the list to your coach or a senior player and compare how they would rate you. Scores that are markedly different are worth reflecting on.

Here is another exercise worth spending time on. The instructions are easy to follow. List four or five of your best performances and record as much detail about them as you can. Allow your mind to remember the sights, sounds, smells and feelings you had before, during and after each successful experience. Really think about these episodes for a few moments and notice how your confidence begins to increase.

You could place some of this information on a small card which you can carry around with you as a quick reminder of your strengths, to recall past successes whenever you feel a bit down.

Self-confidence is based upon realistic self-perception, and will lead to an overwhelming desire to make quality judgements so as to be the best you can be.

Keep your eye on the ball and enjoy a good innings, as I'll teach you about self-talk…

SELF-TALK

My life has been full of terrible misfortunes, most of which never happened.

Michel de Montaigne

Also known as internal dialogue, self-talk is simply the way you talk to yourself inside your head. You worry over a bad innings, congratulate yourself after a good result, even tell yourself how sexy you look in fresh, clean whites. People do it every day, but mostly it's negative. Most people use too much low-energy self-talk. Blaming yourself, chastising yourself. 'I'm not good enough' ... 'I'm too tired' ... 'I'm not able' ... This low-energy talk is one of the major causes of poor performance. If you tell yourself something often enough, you'll begin to believe it. It may not be true, but you will certainly believe it is.

High-energy words promote high-energy thoughts, and unlike the low-energy words, you can practise using high-energy words until your thoughts and emotions adjust for the better. Then your cricket becomes a positive, high-energy experience.

If you have negative beliefs, you have negative self-talk which will confirm the negative beliefs, and so it goes on. You must be aware of your internal dialogue. While positive thinking may not always work, negative thinking almost always does. Put aside any self-pity and accept the responsibility to change. If the voice you use isn't supporting you, change it.

A major problem for sportspeople is repeated dwelling on poor performance. These memories lead to negative self-talk along with emotional discomfort. Your mind may then remember similar bad events. Allowing the past to affect you instead of focusing on the present only slows you down. You suffer tight muscles, energy loss, poor coordination, which all add to the bad performance. Future chapters will show you the techniques to use to get over these poor memories.

Be good to yourself when you talk to yourself by talking positively. Make mental pictures of yourself being a total success. See yourself taking those wickets, hear the congratulations of your teammates and the applause from the spectators and feel how good you feel when you practise being a winner. Mental rehearsal is the next best thing to actually being successful, so do it as often as you can and review it with positive self-talk. You'll be delighted when you see those improvements.

What do you say to yourself when things go wrong?

What do you say to yourself when confronted by a challenge?

The secret is that a confident cricketer will talk differently to himself than one who lacks that confidence, even if they perform equally well. Playing with confidence gives you the security to enjoy every minute and will be reflected by your game. Without that confidence another player may always feel unprepared, nervous, undecided. Those thoughts will then reinforce those beliefs. So you see how vital confident, positive self-talk is.

Self-talk after a good performance:

○ *Confident cricketer – Cricketer lacking confidence*

○ *I am like that – It was luck.*

○ *I always perform like that – It was a one-off*

○ *I'll be the same next time – I can't do that again.*

Self-talk after a poor performance:

○ *Confident cricketer – Cricketer lacking confidence*

○ *It was luck – I am like that.*

○ *It was a one-off – I always perform like that.*

○ *I can't do that again – I'll be the same next time.*

Research tells us that a ratio of three or four positive thoughts to every negative one contributes to better performance. Keep track of the positive or negative thoughts you have about yourself so you can change your negative thinking to a more positive outlook. Any problem you may once have had, when you think of it in the future, how will it make you feel?

Making positive affirmations (self-statements) will help you feel more confident, but to work effectively these affirmations need to be inspiring and practical. Boastful declarations such as 'I am the greatest wicket keeper' or 'nobody can bowl like me' become banana skins as they do not work in the real world and are in fact fruitless, distracting, and eventually you will end up looking foolish. Worse, you will lose confidence and give up using affirmations.

Using affirmations such as 'I am prepared and ready for...' repeated slowly and thoughtfully can lead to calmness, which gives you a positive mindset and leads to clear thinking and good judgement.

You can make things happen with the power of concentration...

CONCENTRATION

When I bat, I block out everything apart from being at one with what I am doing.

Carl Hooper

How do you feel if you have just dropped an important catch? Internally you get angry with yourself, and get down because of the negative experience, while externally you see the look of disappointment on your team-mates' faces, their body language, and maybe hear words of disgruntlement from the spectators.

You feel the odd man out. You have to let it go, then change your mood to perform at your best and not make another mistake. Have you read elsewhere what to do to get yourself into a more upbeat mood?

There is a direct relationship between your breadth of focus and your level of arousal. When arousal is low, you are more concerned with the crowd, bad light, weather conditions, your opponents and other factors going on around you. While with appropriate arousal, you can focus on the moment and ignore all other irrelevant stimuli.

Concentration is one of the easiest skills to master, but one of the most difficult to maintain. The concentration requirements of one day, Twenty20 and especially over several days, vary. Be aware of your concentration skills. Along with the ever-changing variables of an ever-changing game you must know when you have to adopt a less intense soft focus or a more intense focus.

The goal is to be able to control your attention and match the demands of the game. As a batsman standing at the crease, you need to be able to switch your concentration from a broad focus, observing the field positions and boundaries so you know where to hit and place the ball, to a narrow focus, on the seam of the ball and the bowler's hand while maintaining a positive internal focus and avoiding thinking about any other distractions.

As a bowler, you also need a good external focus, using your peripheral vision to know that all your fielders are in their correct positions for the type of ball you are going to deliver, then when running up to bowl, you have to change to a more narrow focus on the line and length of your delivery and be aware of the batsman and the wicket he is guarding.

Internal focusing trades on any mood, sensations, feelings or thoughts. For example, thoughts could be set on being confident or not, on any selectors watching, wondering what your captain thinks about your efforts, facing the first delivery after lunch and still thinking about your lunch, or a message you received on your mobile phone during lunch.

External focusing deals with distractions from people, the location, weather, the pitch being too wet or too dry, blocking out sledging which may cause emotional distraction, bowling the last few overs of the day, all the events outside of yourself.

Concentration varies in duration as it may fluctuate in intensity. Whether you have a narrow or broad span of concentration, whether it is internal or external, the extent of your concentration can harmonise your physical, emotional and mental requirements and successfully focus on the task at hand so you will be distanced from distractions and worries about things beyond your control.

You need to be aware of all the situational changes relating to the run of the match, allowing the most recent happenings to be in focus to the exclusion of anything else. Being 'on the ball' you are able to act instantly with your greatest effectiveness.

Make a personal commitment to improve your concentration. Develop a desire to improve your concentration. Train yourself to shift your focus, and practise when to have a harder or softer focus, which will develop further your concentration skill. Use pre-game preparation to prepare mentally for the game besides warming up the physical skills.

Keep your awareness on tactics and on what you need to do to be focused and ready in any given situation at any moment. Stay relaxed, calm and in your best state to go out to the middle to bat or bowl or when fielding.

What else can you do? Take into consideration the venue, mode of travel and time it takes to get there. You want to arrive early so as not to be rushed and to prepare for the game ahead.

Use concentration exercises by holding the image of the seam of the ball for a few minutes, then looking away.

Breathing exercises and relaxation exercises are covered elsewhere in this book. Use music to increase your arousal, or calm, relaxing sounds to focus and reduce tension.

Use personal triggers and anchors. Think about past rewarding games, maybe against the present opposition and venue. Keep a mental list of previous best performances against them, what you did, how you felt, any great catches, wickets taken. See, hear and feel it all again.

If you're physically prepared, you must also be prepared mentally and emotionally. Set your frame of mind for the game. 'I think I'll bat well today as I'm relaxed, confident, feeling strong' or other good thoughts that can keep you cheerful and make you smile.

Change any mood state and bin less desirable states such as lethargy, tenseness, tiredness which may inhibit you, and think about alertness, calmness and motivation.

Your ability to monitor and evaluate your concentration level will help you have a faster more effective shift of focus and also avoid any potential destructive performance, and will enable optimum performance to occur.

Ego-strengthening will help you catch the next one...

EGO-STRENGTHENING

Form is temporary, class is permanent.

Ian Botham's T-shirt

If you truly want to be a victorious bowler, you must have backbone to keep changing your bowling delivery and field placings to unsettle the batsman and keep him wondering. Be active, not passive. The approach toward ego-strengthening is in the development of your positive inner resources which have come from your positive experiences, including emotions of self-worth, pride and confidence that you feel inside yourself for your efforts in cricket and your life.

Ego-strengthening is important so that, as the optimistic cricketer you are, you have the inner confidence to strive for achievement, along with an increased arousal and the focus to ignore any unnecessary distractions. Even in defeat, an optimistic cricketer will accept failure as something to learn from, examine the failure and create a new plan to win next time around.

A good exercise you can use to demonstrate the power of positive self-talk and develop your ego-strengthening is muscle-testing.

What you do here is create a specific target you would like to reach, let's say a new batting average for example. With the help of a team-mate, standing together, hold your arm out to the side

40

at shoulder height, parallel to the ground and as rigid as possible. Placing one hand on your shoulder, your team-mate will then test to see how much exertion is required to push your arm down about six inches while you resist. This is to make a base measurement of your strength. Your team-mate will then make a series of tests following a verbal statement from you.

First, think and say aloud: 'I don't know whether I will be able to score at least fifty runs [*or whatever your desired target is*] in my next game, but I hope I can.' Your team-mate then applies force to your arm again and notes how much strength is required to bring it down six inches.

Next, you think and say aloud: 'I will try to score at least fifty runs in my next game,' while your team-mate again pushes your arm down to determine if more or less force is required than the first test.

Lastly, you will say aloud and believe: 'I will score at least fifty runs in my next game,' while your team-mate tests your arm strength again.

The test will prove to you that first doubting, then believing as the sentences become more positive, will each time produce a stronger arm than the previous test and you and your team-mate should feel the increased strength as the statements become more positive.

Negative beliefs that do not support you can be buried in your subconscious mind. Testing enables you to find those inner resources you possess; then something unusual but enlightening will occur for you to create lasting change.

To help increase your ego-strengthening, decent, challenging and appropriate goal-setting should not be ignored, along with the positive visualisation exercises you will learn throughout this book.

Are you holding yourself back through perfectionism...?

PERFECTIONISM

I don't care what you say about me, just spell my name right!

P. T. Barnum

A perfectionist can get hung up on themselves doing things perfectly! They can be their own worst enemy because they are never satisfied with their performance. A self-critical perfectionist can never be perfect in their mind because of a fear of making mistakes. That is the greatest barrier to success. Beneath the desire to succeed and reach excellence, a perfectionist often has an ultra-negative, condemning dialogue going on inside their head.

Yes, a perfectionist hates to lose, but a perfectionist must not get anxious about losing.

Some players believe that anything less than perfection is unacceptable. Even when they are playing well they are unable to feel any real fulfilment, as in their eyes they never do anything of a sufficient standard to warrant feelings of personal satisfaction.

As they become discouraged by failing to meet their aspirations, inefficiency, inconsistency, delays and poor results all create a reluctance in a perfectionist to take on new challenges, so they accomplish less rather than adjusting their ambitions realistically. The fear of failure or criticism can make a perfectionist avoid any opportunities to take chances. They may postpone important tasks if the times or situations are not suitable.

Some psychologists believe perfectionists are that way due to parental conditioning. The child's role in life has already been decided, as the parents are living their failed ambition through their child. They want their child to achieve more than they did in their lives. Those rarely satisfied parents who want their offspring to be a sporting success have no idea what they are doing to their child's self-esteem. When they criticise, they are telling their child, or so the child believes, s/he is a failure in their parents' eyes. Children are easily influenced and will develop that fear of failure which can affect them subconsciously for years to come.

However, children coming from a volatile, neglected family life may think that doing everything to perfection will get them reward, recognition, and help them gain control of their unstable environment.

Although perfectionism is not a psychiatric illness, a person's health can be affected by it. Anorexia, obsessive-compulsive disorder, social anxiety or depression can all stem from a darker form of perfectionism. Sufferers are unlikely to seek help as, being perfect, they don't recognise they have any problem.

Do you set high standards for your performance?

Do you feel frustrated if you can't meet your goals?

Do you think that if you don't expect much from yourself you will never be a success?

Is your best never good enough for you?

Are you ever satisfied with your accomplishments?

Do you worry about never measuring up to your ambitions?

Do you believe that dwelling on mistakes is important?

So, when you do well, do you give yourself enough credit? When you do poorly do you beat yourself up? Do you punish yourself if you make a mistake? All cricketers experience failure at some stage; it's how you emotionally handle it that determines if you leave it in the past or recreate it over and over.

Perfectionism damages excellence. Perfectionism does not exist, excellence does. Focus on the things you can control. Put errors behind you, loosen the stays on your self-criticism – let it go! Don't get angry with yourself, move on. Bowling, batting, catching, you can master it all, yet are you master of yourself? Concentrate on what's happening right in front of you, in the present, forget what's just happened – it's history.

You don't have to be perfect at every aspect of cricket to find enjoyment. And besides, team-mates, family, friends might like you more if you have some frailties.

A perfect cricketer is optimistic, do you think he criticises himself…?

THE INNER CRITIC

We don't see things as they are, but rather as we are.

Anaïs Nin

Everybody's a critic and the worst you will ever come across is the one inside your head. This talk has a detrimental effect on your emotional state, even worse than someone in the crowd screaming at you. What does it sound like? Is it angry, sarcastic, resigned? When you make a mistake, I bet you never say, 'Good, that's another learning experience.'

People think because there is a voice inside their head, they must listen to it. You can choose.

It is important to analyse what you do as a cricketer, but relative to the situation. Your criticism should be constructive feedback if it's going to be of any use. If your critical self-talk is not supporting you, play with the direction and tone of the voice. Like many of the methods presented in this manual, this one may seem strange at first. Go give it a shot, you have nothing to lose and everything to gain if it works. Is that reasonable?

Remember when the scoreboard was not ticking over, you were hemmed in by close fielders. You berated yourself for uncertain footwork.

Notice your critical voice with that nasty tone.

Now notice where it is coming from – inside or outside your head? From the front, sides, or back?

If you're right-handed, extend your left arm; if you're left-handed, extend your right.

Stick out the thumb of the extended arm.

Wherever the critical voice came from, imagine you can move it away from your head to your shoulder, then to your elbow, to your wrist, now move it all the way down your arm to the very tip of your thumb.

Hear the voice repeat the same thing, only this time as if you hear the voice coming from the tip of your thumb. Slow it right down, or speed it up. Change it to be like Mickey Mouse, Donald Duck or another cartoon character. Change the tone to something comical.

Move the voice down to your big toe.

You can use another voice to make the negative one shut up.

This technique can also be used on bad memories of someone talking critically to you. You understand this, do you not?

I'll make an interesting comment about critical self-talk. It always takes a hold in the subconscious as a command. So if you tell yourself you're going to make a bad catch, be run out, trip or bowl wide, then it will probably happen. This is because negative self-talk generally has a strong emotion attached to it. A positive suggestion, no matter how good the intention, is usually wishful thinking, and does not contain that emotional content.

If you want to change for the better, pay close attention to the words you use on yourself; they can change the way you perform. Power, timing and placement can get the scoreboard moving for you and when you repeat something with enough emotion, you start to believe it. Use words and phrases that will motivate you and fill you with enthusiasm for the game. I will show you how later. Every sportsperson has two competing voices: one is the negative critic, the other a positive coach. Who you listen to is your choice.

Let's re-programme your self-image…

RE-PROGRAMME YOUR SELF-IMAGE

We are never deceived; we deceive ourselves.

Goethe

Using conscious logical thinking, you know the required response to any game situation. But it's not your conscious mind that manages the response, it's your subconscious which controls your heart rate, breathing, perspiration as well as the emotions of pride, resentment, fear or desire.

To alter any poor memories or attitudes you may have about your game, first weaken them then create better alternatives by using the methods outlined in this book. You're able to go into activities and situations with an abundance of vigour and enthusiasm. Just give yourself time.

Clasp your hands in your usual way, fingers entwined, and notice which thumb is on top. Let go then clasp your hands again in such a way as the opposite thumb is on top. How do you feel? Awkward? Uncomfortable? It doesn't feel natural! The further you go into unfamiliar territory, the greater the psychological discomfort. Your performance may suffer temporarily as you make needed adjustments to your game, but change does that. If you were to place your hands and thumbs the 'awkward' way every time, it would eventually feel natural, as will your adjustments to your game.

You have talent. Can you adjust to a new team or league? This method will show you how to perform with confidence.

Take a deep breath, sit back and relax as you exhale.

Tighten, then relax all your muscle groups.

Recall the sights, sounds, feelings of you performing at your very best.

In your mind's eye imagine another you standing in front of you. This is the best that you have ever been, or ever will be, at the top of your game, every decision you make is the right one.

If you can't see it or imagine it, just know that it's there.

When you feel happy with the image in front of you, notice the way you stand, move, hit, bowl, catch.

Notice a confident champion before you, bowling a good length ball every time, an unstoppable batsman or a superb wicketkeeper.

Now step into your image and see through those eyes, hear through those ears, and feel how good it feels to be that living image.

Keep that important feeling and make everything bigger, brighter, more powerful. Let it glow.

You can step into a more intense image of yourself. Do that several times, getting bigger and brighter and stronger each time.

Take a few minutes, if you wish, to imagine yourself in any situation from the past where you want a bad memory changed to a positive outcome, or see yourself in a future situation dominating play, being rewarded, excelling. You can, you know, forget about ever having had that problem.

Daydream and know it can come true.

Think of a future situation or event when having a positive feeling will be desired. Take tail-end batting. You've read the routine above, give it a go, or try this one next.

The Circle of Excellence exercise builds a positive mood and creates a state of mind which will be useful in the future. In front of you, create a Circle of Excellence. This represents that state you require. Imagine it has a colour, maybe there is a sound there. This circle brings for you all the skills and positive assurance you want.

Now, return to a time when you had that positive resource, or imagine you had the right attitude, dedication and grit.

Take a deep breath, exhale…

Step into the memory inside the circle.

Imagine the bright colour shining down and all around, going into every cell of your body, from the top of your head, all the way down to the tips of your toes. Double the brightness.

Tell yourself you are more confident, talented, fitter.

Every breath you take, you take in more of the resource; you're demoralising the fielders.

Stop.

Take a step back, away from the circle, and shake yourself off.

Choose a special word that will have meaning for you, or a sound.

Again step into the circle and this time say or think the special word, hear that sound.

Imagine that feeling you have getting stronger, being absorbed by your body; strength and enthusiasm glow from you. You're more tenacious, hanging around the crease, you're under no pressure, all your runs are a bonus to your team. If you can see it in your mind's eye, you can achieve it.

You can do the Circle of Excellence just about anywhere. Rehearse first; then, going onto the playing field, imagine the circle before you just before stepping onto the pitch. Do it as you take position at the wicket, before you turn to start your run to bowl. How about stepping out of the shower. Getting out of a car. Overcome problems or challenges with this technique before they occur.

Feeling good? You're learning to master your emotions…

MASTER YOUR EMOTIONS

No matter how thin you slice it, there are always two sides.

Baruch Spinoza

You keep coming back for more now, don't you! Any unpleasant thought you have comes with an unpleasant feeling. If you want to win the game going on inside your head, you have to deal with your emotions. In just a moment I'm going to guide you to be your most confident self and feel resourceful for any endeavour you choose.

You will encounter a broad range of emotions naturally during a cricket match which may predict the performance you are going to have. By being aware and monitoring your emotions you can become aware of your optimal performance state.

You may be wondering: what is an emotion? An emotion is the mood you are in at any particular moment and is individual and unique to all of us. Love, hate, confidence, fear, they are all emotions and we constantly go in and out of them all day long. All behaviour is the result of an emotion.

Remember times when you were filled with confidence, determination, joy, optimism. How about that passion you feel for cricket? Unfortunately, you also suffered anger, sadness and resentment. Emotions are your subconscious mind's way of telling you there is something going on you should pay attention to.

It's useful to take a brief look at emotions for you to gain more insight. A primary emotion occurs close to the event that brings it on, so it is the emotion we feel first. A secondary emotion appears after the primary emotion. So you could feel joy as a primary emotion, that will lead to bliss or delight, pride, optimism.

Sometimes the problem with primary emotions is that they disappear as fast as they arrive, to be replaced by secondary emotions which can complicate matters as they may come from a more complex chain of thinking, so they can make it difficult to really know what is going on, as in the case of anger arriving out of fear.

There are many possible primary negative emotions and some psychologists may use a different list of primary and secondary emotions.

Here you'll learn how to programme yourself to experience more of the resourceful emotions you want in all the situations you want. The pictures you make in your imagination and the way you talk to yourself are known as internal representations. And that's all they are, representations, not real life, so they cannot harm you.

Changes in breathing, muscle tension, posture, even facial expression, all caused by emotion, influence your feelings and behaviour, as you may now appreciate.

Think of a time when you felt nervous, anxious, defeated. Notice how it affects your posture, your shoulders slump and your head may have dropped.

I can show you a simple way to change. Wherever you are, plant your feet firmly on the ground, hold yourself tall, pull your shoulders back, take a great big breath, let it out, look up at the ceiling or the sky and put a great big grin on your face. Smile with your whole face with feeling. Now try to remember that tense situation again. People cannot be anxious when they are smiling. Notice your mood has probably lifted and you no longer remember it in the same unpleasant way.

Why not keep the feeling there? Stand straight, let your spine support you while you imagine a bright golden thread running up your spine and straight out to the sky. Let yourself relax, held up by this golden thread.

If your body is tense, it is producing different chemicals than when it is relaxed. Your heart rate may increase, or your blood pressure, so you feel and think differently than you do when you are relaxed. See how making physiological changes makes a difference to your emotional response.

Here is a way to increase awareness of your optimal performance state so you can play well. Think about the best and worst game you have played and choose two to five emotions that you experienced during each match; you may have been motivated during your best performance and overaggressive during your worst.

Take each emotion you experienced during those two games and scale the intensity of each one between zero and ten, with zero being nothing at all and ten being the top of the scale. You can use this method to monitor all your future games as well. When complete, consider these issues:

1. *What have you noticed regarding the way your emotions affect your performance?*

2. *How can this information be used in your next game to ensure playing at your best?*

3. *What helped or stopped you from accessing the optimal intensity of your emotions?*

4. *Are there any emotions present that are not as important as you first thought?*

5. *Are there any emotions you need to include?*

Notice the important link between self-awareness and cricket performance, and how this awareness gives you an understanding of yourself and may help you predict how you play your next game in a great mood rather than a negative, destructive one. That next game could be an important one.

And there's a lot said about pressure…

PRESSURE & STRESS

When you have fun, it changes all the pressure into pleasure.

Ken Griffeyn

Pressure gets a bad name. It's the ultimate lie detector. When it's present it can be a positive force, bringing out the best in you, or a negative one, being an excuse to quit. Some cricketers will break through, while those less committed break down. Everyone feels pressure in competition, no one is immune. It can often start long before the game starts. Cricketers under pressure become internally self-conscious rather than externally task-conscious. Worrying about making a mistake will usually get you one.

Recall a time when you felt pressure. A short-pitched bounce coming at you like a thunderbolt? Remember what you were doing, feeling, saying. Were you excited or nervous? Did you expect failure or feel a desire to win? Did you let all kinds of negative thoughts come into your mind which may have been influenced by personality or environmental factors?

Excessive mental pressure often produces mental blocks. Then anything recently learnt in training, be it technical or tactical, may well be forgotten. Some situations can be embarrassing or humiliating, especially in front of team-mates or a crowd, creating a negative performance experience. These experiences lodge themselves in the mind and body, showing up as performance problems right away, or lying dormant for days, weeks or months before raising their ugly heads.

Demands on players are higher than ever the higher you go. Sponsorship, money, TV exposure, fans; all increase the pressure. Become mentally tough, look at pressure as a challenge to drive yourself that much harder.

Pressure and stress create muscle tension, causing over-tightness, generally in the neck and shoulders. The heart rate goes up, breathing quickens, skin perspires. Some feel their stomachs churn. These are all physical early warning signs. Mentally your mind starts racing, negative thoughts come floating into your mind.

Pressure or stress on players involved in cricket – long game duration, rain stoppage, being away from family, frustration from an umpire's decision, under-performance, team upsets – can all lead to the debilitating and exhausting state of depression. Then the players' thoughts will revolve around loss and will have persistent negative images of themselves performing poorly.

Depression is a very strong emotion and is on the increase as the number one psychological disorder of the western world. Negative thinking makes it difficult for someone depressed to activate or motivate themselves. There is a chapter on depression later on.

Did you know there is a relationship between mood and food? Foods high in refined sugars, such as fizzy drinks, chocolate bars or biscuits, can increase blood sugar levels very quickly, then give a false high. When those effects dissolve, you quickly feel down, fatigued, with poor concentration, due to your body and muscle groups using up the refined sugars too quickly. What you need is food which gives a slower, more natural release and assists your mood, like bananas and raisins, to avoid the physical feelings of pressure.

Stress is a much-used word but a misunderstood condition. It kicks in whenever you are threatened in any way. The sympathetic nervous system (SNS) pumps more adrenaline and cortisol into the heart, along with extra blood and oxygen to your muscles for the 'fight or flight' response which helps you combat or escape from danger.

This is balanced by your parasympathetic nervous system (PNS): your blood pressure drops and you relax, which helps you to digest your food. Both these systems work together.

When you're stressed one of the systems (SNS) does too much and the other system (PNS) is not being employed enough. Your nervous system cannot tell the difference between a real or an imagined event. So if you are suffering an emotional threat you are still producing the same stress chemicals as your body needs to fight or flee.

As those chemicals have been pumped into your system in response to thoughts you cannot fight or flee from, your body has no way to get rid of them and over time, if it is a regularly occurring event, the build-up of these stress chemicals can cause illness and disease.

When you're tense, you want to get your task over as soon as possible. Mentally your mind races. The more you hurry, the worse you will probably play, making mistakes, creating even more pressure and greater muscle tension, so wasting more energy. Consider this. Stress is strictly internal, it does not exist outside the player's mind. Match conditions do not become anxious, only players do.

Poise under pressure will be admired by many. They wonder how you do it. It's important to realise that cricket creates a certain amount of stress in every serious participant. It is useful to recognise and become familiar with your own unique mixture of emotional reactions and physical tendencies that appear during stressful times. Increased heart rate, muscle tension, loss of appetite, sweaty palms, impatience, irritability. How do you cope with it?

One effective method is simply to write down specific stressors. The simple act of recording a behaviour you wish to change leads to improvement in the required direction.

Use travel time to listen to inspirational audiotapes or CDs. Hearing a person you admire and respect can have a positive impact on your mood. Upbeat music can make the miles fly by; or maybe something soothing to keep you calm en route.

Stop reading this chapter right now and do the following breathing exercise. Close your eyes and take a deep breath down into your abdomen. Count to three as you inhale through your nose and count to four as you exhale through your mouth. Do it five times. Notice that if you pay close attention to your breathing and counting, you should, after five breaths, begin to feel more relaxed.

You can even enhance that deep breathing technique by remembering a time when you were on top of your game. As you breathe and focus on the picture, say to yourself a word or phrase that can represent the relaxed feeling. 'Steady' or 'easy' might do. Play around and notice what works for you. Psychological research has shown deep breathing while reciting a simple word or phrase weakens even severe stress considerably.

You can do that anytime. You may feel daft doing it surrounded by team-mates, but put it this way: they may well be as nervous or stressed as you so they do not notice what you are doing and even if they do, they may follow your example in decreasing their own stress.

There are some keys you can use to remain calm. Think about best batting, bowling or fielding performances, past achievements and successes from using your skills and the good feelings they created. Stop any negative thinking as soon as you are aware of it and use your imagination to think about your strengths and resources. Remember good moods and things that make you smile. Focus outwards on pleasures, physical activity, problem-solving, improving relationships on and off the pitch.

Days before an important game, a trial, appearing before selectors, a little nervousness may creep in. So actually the game begins before the game begins. At home, the journey to the venue, in the changing room. How do you reduce pressure and place your mind in the here and now? Here's one method to give yourself an advantage. When you arrive in the changing room, use each article of clothing you remove – jacket or blazer, shirt, trousers, one shoe, then the other – to let go of a concern or irrational fear. Each article of kit you put on, imagine you're putting on resources of relaxation, courage or resilience. By the time you have changed, any distraction you were focused on will have dissolved. Now you're in the right time zone and in the best state of mind for what's ahead.

Let's see how you can drive away the spectre of anger…

ANGER & PSYCHING

Learn to control your emotions or they will control you.
Edgar Martinez

Anger is born out of frustration and expectation. It feeds on itself. When you allow anger to get the better of you, it generally brings out the worst in you. As emotions go up, your capacity to behave in a calm, reasoned manner goes down. Anger blocks concentration, tactics and technique. Your temper can hurt your team-mates, they will find it difficult to trust you and you may despise yourself later for being so destructive.

Do you let opponents or situations tie you up in knots? Your heart beats faster, your breathing quickens. You stand there, all clenched jaw, staring eyes and hunched-up shoulders and arms, hacked off and out of control. Or you can learn from it.

You control your moods and emotions. If someone makes you angry, you're giving that person power over you. They are then controlling your moods and emotions.

Anger can often be fear in disguise, a reaction to inner fears, as anger is based on insecurity. Non-violent fighting spirit is based on self-confidence.

Cricketers who cannot control their anger will never make great players. They hit the ball with their egos, not the bat. The best have the maturity to master their emotions, not to be servants to them. That emotional energy allows you to raise your game. Many sportspeople can channel anger positively as it motivates them. Rushes of blood kept under control will work for you.

In every game comments are made. Short leg could be having a go, slip could be having a go. A fast spin bowler is staring you right in the eye and having a go. It's easy to lose focus and get out next ball. When you're at the crease and focused it just becomes background chatter.

You cannot have a blind rage of anger if you remain calm. If you have an anger button, there is something you can do about it. While you are reading this get yourself relaxed as we are going to set a calm button as a resource before another anger moment arrives. For convenience, we will set the 'anchors' to either side of your waist, so you could do this standing up during a game, and with it being inconspicuous, nobody will have a clue what you are doing. There is a detailed chapter on anchoring techniques later.

Close your eyes and think of a recent time when you lost your cool, or think about the things that may trigger anger for you on a regular basis. Now just for a few moments, really get back into it, get fully immersed into that experience, see everything you saw, hear everything you heard to make you angry, feel exactly the way you felt.

Now step out of the experience as if you are watching someone else (dissociated) and rewind the scene as if you were rewinding a video until you reach the very first moment your anger began to develop. Go back a couple more frames, or seconds if that is easier, and imagine somewhere on your body a very large red button, let's say your left waist.

Open your eyes and say your phone number to break state, then close your eyes again.

Now take three deep breaths, exhaling out longer than the in breath. Think of a relaxing time, a good holiday, being on a beach, a quiet walk beside a lake, or a fun moment. Where do you feel that feeling? Let it spread throughout your body, going up to the top of your head and down to the tips of your toes, see it as a colour, feel it as a wonderful feeling, or hear it as a sound.

As it begins to peak, imagine a big green or blue button at your right waist. Press this several times and let the feelings get bigger.

Open your eyes. Repeat your telephone number to break state. Now press your red button and immediately after, press your green/ blue button and hold them both for a moment before releasing your red button while continuing to hold the other.

Repeat the sequence another half-dozen times until triggering your green/blue button automatically creates a calm response.

Psyching or gamesmanship comes with the territory. Cheating, provocation, verbal abuse, lies, are all designed to upset you emotionally and disrupt your concentration. Recognise it for what it is and don't allow sledging to get inside your head and ruin your composure. If it affects you it's there, at the back of your mind. Even if you pretend it doesn't bother you, it does. Your answer should be 'Ha, so you're the challenge!'

Be also aware there are two kinds of psyching – one your opponent does and the one you do to yourself. Some players believe they can only perform when they are psyched up and that a calm, relaxed attitude would feel the wrong approach.

Come closer my friend. A way to divert over-arousal is to divert your attention. Develop a ritual when you need to calm yourself or when you need a few moments to get yourself together. Pick a spot or a mark on the field or around the ground. Between each play walk to that mark and touch it, or if that's not possible, look at it. This strategy can keep your mind focused while you give yourself a pep talk.

Do something physical to slow events down for yourself. Rub your hands together, tie your laces, rub the bat, bounce the ball. Nothing too complicated. These are all small psychological boosts for mental and emotional management. When you can, change into a dry shirt, fresh socks, put on a sweat band. Do some small change to make things feel like it's a new start.

Don't get in a spin with the umpire even if he is as blind as a bat and as deaf as a post. Accept any decision and get on with the game, he will not change his mind. It all evens itself out in the end anyway. If it's a bad pitch, the umpire will have more difficult decisions to make.

You could always do unto others as they do to you and be as confrontational. Often they can't take it. You're now taking the initiative, but do you really need to lower yourself to their level? The best response is to be mature and have compassion for someone who has to resort to gamesmanship to defeat you as they can't do it through talent alone. Intimidation, but not malice, is part of the game as long as you are not deliberately trying to hurt someone. You're a fast bowler, they have a bat, that's all there is to it!

What else can you do with the emotional charge of aggravation or frustration? Here are some more options you can do and what to avoid:

○ *Deep breathing has always been one answer besides counting to ten. Take six deep breaths, then take six more, in through your nose and out through your mouth.*

○ *There is no need to let emotional episodes or rash behaviour become a pattern. If you keep losing it, be mature enough to look for assistance.*

○ *You can realise that the crisis is only temporary, it's not going to end your cricket career.*

○ *Your objective is to become a better cricketer, your response to a crisis should help, not destroy, your future.*

○ *Remember, anger and frustration happen to everyone, not just you. Leave your bad emotions behind and get back into optimum performance mode as soon as you can.*

○ *Avoid doing anything or making decisions until you regain your composure. Angry, you will be more impulsive and may do something you regret later.*

○ *If you make foolish mistakes with over-excited feelings, take action to calm yourself and cultivate your mental strength rather than playing Russian roulette.*

Let's calm ourselves with breathing…

BREATHING

They can because they think they can.

Virgil

Often overlooked, correct breathing should be carried out at all times, not only when you feel tense, as it calms your body and mind. When you breathe normally, your body is unconsciously maintaining the balance of oxygen and carbon dioxide. When you're apprehensive, breathing changes to fast and shallow. This causes dizziness, poor vision, tiredness, breathlessness, which only increases anxiety further.

If you practise correct breathing, it becomes second nature, so you must breathe properly when you're anxious, it will help keep you 'grounded'.

High, or clavicular, breathers only breathe into the upper portion of the chest and lungs so only a small amount of air can enter. Stale air remains in the lower lungs and impurities are not properly expelled from the body. You can notice these people always seem to be gulping or gasping for breath.

Most people breathe into the chest for mid, or intercostal, breathing. This is still not efficient as the lower chest is only partially expanded.

With low, or abdominal, breathing you take in good qualities of air and you are expelling impurities from your lungs.

Where do you breathe?

Lie on your back. Place one hand on your chest and the other on your abdomen. Breathe out to empty your lungs. Now breathe in your normal fashion. Don't force it as you may get light-headed, in which case give it a rest till you feel better.

Which hand rises and falls the most? Is it the one on your chest? Well you're not breathing deeply enough. You should be breathing into your abdomen. Here's how. Breathe in through your nose and out through your mouth. Imagine a position an inch or two below your navel and that you're sending the breath you breath down to it. You should feel your stomach area swell as you inhale. If it doesn't, place something light, like a paperback book, on your abdomen and as you inhale, concentrate on making it rise.

When you breathe into the chest you are only filling your lungs about three-quarters, the bottom quarter being stale air. Breathing into the abdomen actually fills the bottom of the lungs with fresh, rich air. Now to completely fill all of your lungs, as you expand your abdomen, pull back your shoulders and head to fully fill the top part.

Oxygen is energy. It helps relax the muscles and gives clarity of mind. When you hold your breath you create pressure and a nervous feeling develops. Slow, deep breathing improves the quality of your blood, will make you feel relaxed and you can do it anywhere, keeping your body and mind in the present.

When you look at the mechanics of breathing, you realise that holding your breath the moment you carry out any physical exertion instead of exhaling is completely wrong. It places your body under more strain and your energy is kept in rather than being released. Naturally exhaling while exerting movement allows for more accuracy hitting the ball, and you feel your muscles working in the follow-through, enabling you to put more distance on the ball, or during the moment of delivery when you are bowling.

Feeling more comfortable? You're ready to experience something new about relaxation…

RELAXATION

Our bodies are our gardens, our wills are gardeners.
William Shakespeare

Some think of relaxation as sitting in front of the TV, going to the pub, spending time with family or friends. These may be relaxing times, but they still require a degree of emotional, mental and physical stimulation. True relaxation is a moment of emotional, mental and physical quiet. Your breathing and heart-rate slow, your muscles relax and you feel calm and at peace in your body.

Here I will describe progressive relaxation, which is basically a relaxation routine where you start from the top of your head and work all the way down through your various muscle groups. Progressive relaxation was developed by Dr Edmund Jacobson in the 1920s as a way a person could consciously relax. It was an effective but slow process and other therapists such as Richard Suinn and then Herbert Benson developed ways of speeding it up. It is a proven, simple way of relaxing the body and mind.

Relaxation itself is valuable to health as it relieves mental and physical tension. When both your body and mind are at ease, other mental skills become unlocked, then your progress toward mental training, self-esteem, goal-setting and concentration will be smoothly accomplished.

Close your eyes if you want.

Take a deep breath and clench a fist tightly and hold for three seconds, imagining the tension in the fist as a colour, light or electricity, something which will represent the tension for you.

Relax your fist as you exhale slowly. Imagine the muscle tension as a change of colour – light blue or green can work well – or change the substance, feel it dissolving or melting away. Notice the difference in your hand before and after it was clenched and the relaxation you should feel now.

Do the same with your other hand and in the future, you can clench both hands at the same time.

Breathe in slowly, carry on with the muscles of both arms, really tense them, imagine the colours or shapes, however you imagine the tension to be, then release and exhale as the colour or shape changes. Let the arms relax and enjoy the feeling.

What other part of your body do you think we'll relax next?

On to your face. Really scrunch your face up and notice how good it feels when you relax it.

Shrug your shoulders, hold, then go through the relaxation procedure. Just let go.

Next your chest and back, start to feel like a rag doll.

Now on to your waist.

Proceed to your hips and buttocks, tense and relax them.

As you breathe out, you might think about the feelings in your legs. Tense your thighs, let them go. Feel yourself sinking into the floor.

The calf muscles getting loose and limp, sinking down.

Finally your feet, all tension draining away.

Isn't it interesting how your body relaxes without trying too hard? Enjoy the feeling of calm. You can go through this exercise as many times as you wish, just notice how relaxed you feel at the end.

You are able to do that quickly. Tense and relax the upper body as a whole, then the lower body, then the legs. Fielders need to relax between balls to keep themselves fresh mentally. Fielding on the boundary, you get a detached view where you could notice a flaw in the batsman's game, any little nervous movements before and after the ball is delivered. Wicket keepers can use physical relaxation to stay alert while the bowler is walking away before turning to start his run.

You can utilise this relaxed state by making positive suggestions to yourself.

Another way to do this is without tensing the muscles, perhaps just before sleep as you lie in bed, as physically tensing your muscles may keep you awake. Imagine a wave of relaxation soothing its way down through your body; maybe it's a soft colour, one that can really relax you, going into every fibre of your body. Remember a time and place of peace, a sanctuary perhaps or gazing at the stars on a clear summer evening or lying on the beach, hearing the waves gently lap on the sea shore. Engage in the moment.

How about active relaxation? I'll illustrate this with a story. Several members of a team were told to sprint eight hundred metres as fast as they could, the time was recorded. Next, the coach instructed them to sprint the same distance, only this time at just ninety percent of effort. Their time was better the second time. Why? Your muscles are organised into opposing pairs. Running, along with many other activities, is performed most effectively when some muscles are contracting while others are relaxing. While sprinting at top speed, you use all of your leg muscles, so they are actually working against themselves, accelerating and braking at the same time. This prevents you running as fast as you can. As a paradox, when running at ninety percent effort you are relaxing the muscles enough to stop them hindering maximum effort.

The same can be said about bowling. Trying to bowl as hard as you can uses all the muscles in the arm – especially the biceps and triceps – so they are working against themselves. It's a bit like 'Ready, fire, aim!' To achieve accuracy and speed, the biceps need to relax, while the triceps do the work for you so you get 'Ready, aim, fire!'

Here's an ideal way to produce instant, physical relaxation which comes from yoga. Breathe through your eyes. That's right. Imagine that as you inhale, the air you're breathing is entering your body through your eyes. You can actually feel your muscles relax if your eyes are open, or shut. It happens all by itself!

Now you know how to relax and use your imagination, let's see how you ask questions...

CREATIVE QUESTIONS

If you fail to plan, you plan to fail.

John Wooden

Asking questions is about the easiest and one of the most powerful tools you can use to transform yourself for the better and challenge your mind.

Questions direct your focus of attention. If your spin bowling is poor, notice how you question your spin bowling ability. Simply ask yourself, 'How can I ask this in a positive way?' which makes your questions more empowering.

Many sportspeople get frustrated because they ask themselves negative questions. 'Why can't I…?' To understand the question, your mind automatically looks for the reason why you cannot. But no matter what the answer is, you are still accepting the fact that you cannot do it. You're also reinforcing the problem in your mind. Here's a trick. Change 'why' into 'how'. Ask yourself 'How can I do this?' This assumes it can be done and there can be a number of ways it can be done, so the question allows your mind to search out a positive solution.

You'll be surprised to discover how you can go further. You might ask, 'How should I train in the nets today?' Instead ask, 'How should I train in the nets today to enjoy every minute?'

So, ask questions that focus on the positive:

○ *How can this stamina problem be solved easily?*

○ *How many different ways can I guard against batting faults?*

○ *How can I stop inconsistent run-up?*

○ *How am I going to become…?*

These questions put your brain into a more resourceful state. If you're not happy with an answer, change the way you ask the question.

Here's another one for you. When you want the answer to something, ask yourself the question about ten times and notice what you come up with. Your brain will keep searching until a happy solution is found. It's good to know that your unconscious has the answer to all the questions you'll ever ask. You can allow fresh answers to come to you.

Ask yourself these:

○ *Can you identify your ideal cricket role?*

○ *Do you love the game so much you'd pay to play it?*

○ *What difference would it make if you could improve ten to twenty percent?*

○ *How passionate do you feel about cricket? Bowling, batting, fielding?*

○ *What would you do if you had unlimited ability?*

Curiosity creates questions. By bringing your vivid imagination into play as you ask creative questions, you build up a vivid representation of the answer, then amplify it, make it a sensory-rich experience, turn the colours brighter, the sounds louder, the feelings stronger. By regularly concentrating on what you want, you condition your mind to attract more of it.

If you ever find it hard to bring an answer to mind, remember the solution to it! Remembrance was an old philosophers' trick. Instead of asking your mind to search for an answer to a challenge, simply ask your mind to remember it. Again the presupposition that you once knew the answer creates a mindset that the answer actually exists, so eliminates the anxiety of helplessness you may endure.

Many apprehensions and worries are often caused by not giving your mind something better to do. Look at it this way, the one asking the question is usually the one holding the cards.

You may find decision-making even more interesting with this method developed by Yvonne Oswald. How do you feel when you cannot make up your mind about a choice you have to make? It becomes frustrating, I know. Begin to apply this strategy to small daily decisions and build up to more important ones. Your subconscious understands your needs (not your wishes) much better than you do consciously.

How to ask a question is important for clear decision-making, so set it like this: 'How good is it for me to…?' which is far better to ask than 'Do I want to…?' When you have a decision to make, ask a question that gives you a number between zero and ten, such as 'How good is it for me to take up yoga for more flexibility?' The quicker you come up with an answer, the more you can place trust in your intuition. If the answer that emerges from any question is five or less, take the answer as a NO.

Ask yourself this: 'How good is my team for me right now?' If your answer is five or below, start looking elsewhere as the team is not taking you anywhere.

Other ways to ask questions are 'How likely is it that...?' or 'How good for me is...?'

What if you have a choice on bowling a leg spin or a straight yorker at leg and middle? You could come up with an answer of three and eight, so go for the yorker.

Test this out first to find out how much your subconscious mind is in touch by asking a true or false question such as 'Is my name Bill?' and notice what number between zero and ten reveals itself.

Good answers from good questions often come to you through rest...

REST

The ancestor of every action is a thought.

Ralph Waldo Emerson

When we do sports, especially competitive sports, there is often damage caused to the body because the will to fight and the will to win makes the body tense and then illness and injuries mount up.

Both your mind and body have their own way to rest and recharge their batteries. This happens about every ninety minutes when they stop external focus and spend around fifteen minutes to rest and replenish. This is known as the ultradian rhythm, when you find yourself daydreaming and a soft feeling of comfort begins in your body. People constantly ignore these signs so go into overload. If you go with it, you will feel refreshed and have better concentration after.

Deepen the experience by self-hypnosis, meditation, or listening to relaxing music. Imagine yourself in a favourite place, an exotic beach, an oasis of peace and calm, a garden, somewhere that is special for you. Your nervous system can't tell the difference between a real or an imagined event, so fool it into believing it's on holiday.

Do this exercise to improve well-being once or twice a day; it doesn't take long and is a variation on the relaxation exercise I described earlier.

Put your attention on your feet and notice any feeling in them, coldness, warmth, weight.

Take a deep breath and as you exhale, imagine a warm, pleasant feeling begin in your feet. You can imagine a colour.

When you're ready take another deep breath and imagine that warm, relaxed feeling travelling up to your knees. As it does, say a word like 'relax', 'rest', 'peace', or give each stage a number. Let that comfortable feeling penetrate your muscles and bones, soothing them.

When you're ready, take another gentle breath and imagine the feeling rising up to your waist and repeat your special word or the next number.

With the same breathing pattern, let that feeling of ease and relaxation arrive at your shoulders, soothing them as you say your special word.

Next let that relaxation flow from your shoulders down your arms and into your hands and fingers.

Again breathe and let the feeling flow all the way up your face to the top of your head. Say the word or number and let the feeling spread all over your body.

In your mind say the word and imagine the relaxation doubling and floating down from your head so it mixes with those good feelings already going on inside your body.

As this relaxation drifts down your body, imagine any tension being washed down and away out of your feet so it makes room for new, refreshing energy spreading down from your head, until you feel your body glow with energy from your head to your feet.

Now take a few moments to really bask in that feeling of relaxation.

If you want, do it again. The more you practise, the better it becomes.

Just allow whatever happens to happen and feel satisfied with what you're accomplishing.

Maybe you will think about goals…

GOALS

*People are not lazy. They simply have impotent goals –
that is, goals that do not inspire them.*

Anthony Robbins

Can't get enough now, can you? A goal is a mental representation of something you wish to achieve within a given time frame. Aiming for goals is a simple way to keep yourself motivated, evaluate progress, create emotion and achieve things. A goal can give you clearer direction. If you don't know where you're going, you'll probably end up somewhere else. Talent will take you just so far. Setting goals goes with mental training and hard work.

People don't plan to fail, they fail to plan. What would you do if you knew you could not fail? Goals can stop you stumbling through life. Why leave things to chance? Goals can help you move away from your limitations. Goals can make you the team's number one pace bowler. Setting goals is an art. By focusing your mind on a target you are more likely to achieve it. If you don't aim for goals, your efforts will go wide.

A well known acronym for setting goals is **SMART**. The **S** is for Specific. The more specific you make the goal, the easier it will become to figure out if you are on target and when you have achieved it. Bring in your senses when you form your goal so you can see, hear and feel everything as you visualise yourself achieving your desired outcome. Be careful about specifics. 'I want to score fifty runs a game' is specific. What happens when you've chalked up your fifty? 'OUT' can be heard. 'I want to score more than fifty runs a game' gets you a good innings and gives you room to go further.

M is Measurable. Create a starting-point from where you can measure your improvements.

A stands for Achievable. High enough to inspire solid hope of reaching it. Only you or your coach know if your goal is achievable. Is it too challenging or not challenging enough?

R is Realistic. Do you have the personal resources and skills to bring about your goal? Would more training be required? If your goal is too big, too outlandish, too far away, it can damage your motivation.

And **T** is Time-bound, an accomplishment date. If you do not set some form of deadline, tomorrow never comes. Keep it flexible as reaching the goal is the important element, not the time frame. Keep on reassessing your goal until it is reached. Make goals challenging. A goal is a dream with a target.

Hesitation ruins action. Stop putting things off, as with action, you can aim for bigger, juicier goals. What do you want to accomplish in cricket? It starts when you set goals. It's the first step into putting your dreams into action.

Ask goal-oriented questions:

o   *What do you want from cricket? Is it specific, definite, measurable?*

o   *Can you maintain your goal?*

o   *What stops you having that goal?*

o   *What resources have you? Are they emotional, financial, mental, physical, spiritual?*

o   *What resources are required?*

On a scale of zero to ten, what would ten be like as your very best? What would two be like? What's the closest to ten you've been? Where are you on that scale now? What would it take to go two points higher? I bet you can do twice as well as you're doing.

How you design your goals makes a big difference. The bigger the better. Your goal should excite and scare you at the same time. If it frightens you, you are facing your fear of failure, but you're not backing down. Set your goals in concrete. 'I'll do my best' or 'We'll see how it goes' do not carry much enthusiasm.

Break the ultimate goal down into smaller parts until each step is easy for you to take. Having a number of smaller chunks to work on stops you freaking out over a large overwhelming one. State goals with joy and act as if they were already a reality. Read or recite your goal every day. Your mind needs constant repetitions to accept your aims deeply and unconsciously. Be consistent.

When you set your sights on a goal wholeheartedly, your subconscious will do what it can to help you reach it. It doesn't take much to get things started, a simple thought or action. Or even better, a thought and action combined.

Here's one goal you should aim for. Learn the Laws of Cricket, particularly the LBW and No Ball rules. It's important that you totally understand these as they have an influence on your performance.

Effective goals do several things. Higher goals lead to higher expectation. Conventional wisdom is right in suggesting we generally get what we expect. So if you set a modest goal, do not expect a high-level result.

Goals give direction toward positive outcomes, and more importantly, they can concentrate your efforts so as to avoid distractions.

Goals give you growth. They can transform your life. Grab any evidence that shows you are achieving your target or that motivates you. Hold it in your hands, smell it, let it shine on you. Expect that standing ovation.

Lack of accurate feedback causes more goals to fail than any other reason. Your goals can be specific, organised, realistic, but you need information indicating the progress toward your target. Have some checkpoints to evaluate your progress. Include target dates when you will evaluate your progress and recommit to your present goals, or create new ones. As the season unfolds, goals will guide, inspire and motivate.

One of the main reasons why players do not reach a desired goal is they do not have a goal beyond it. Your goal becomes more motivational when other possibilities are likely once you have achieved it.

I must highlight the value of having realistic expectations and specific goals to aim for. The magic begins when you set goals. Make a list of what you want. Write everything down. This is the first step to putting your dreams into action and turning them into reality.

However you are getting on, rejoice when you reach about three quarters of your goal to celebrate how far you have come and remain upbeat.

I cover more on goals in the 'Self-Hypnosis For Cricket' section which comes later.

Let's change any negative self-talk by reframing…

REFRAMING

Failure is an opportunity to begin again more intelligently.

Henry Ford

Failure is not the end result. Some people see failure as an excuse to give up, others think about failure so much, it becomes the best way to repeat it. Others, you included, can see things in a positive light by reframing any situation. The glass becomes half-full, never half-empty. You are in control. Reframing gives you the flexibility to make situations work for you.

In training, do you think you may never reach the required level? Do you worry you will lose the next game? Thoughts like these hamper performance. If you're afraid of losing, your dominant thought is about losing. Winners think about the next game and how to win it, losers think about the last one and who to blame. Notice your thoughts and change them to positives.

When you come across an opponent who is bigger, fitter, faster, more experienced than you, don't tell yourself s/he is better than you. Use your internal dialogue to put the person down, ridicule them. Play on any weakness, real or perceived. Change their appearance – remember how to do that from the 'Imagination' chapter earlier? This gives your mind something to do and gives you the confidence to face them. More relaxed, you can focus more easily on your strategy and stop any self-talk of fear or tension.

Positive thinking helps you realise that there are limitations in any opponent's ability, as explained in the 'Imagination' chapter. If your opponent is larger than you, tell yourself: 'Being bigger s/he will be too slow or clumsy, there's no way s/he is going to keep up with me, I'm more agile, slimmer, faster.'

If your opponent is smaller, maybe faster than you, it's probable s/he will be physically weaker. 'I'm stronger, I'll hit the ball all over the field.' Look for their weaknesses, not strengths, and create emotion when you speak to yourself: be elated, believe you have the skill to defeat your opponent.

Know that if you play with performance-damaging thoughts, you are able to change or remove them. To make any negative emotion disappear, amend the thought. Change any colour, put a frame around it, make it smaller, further away, make it darker. Move the sound, change it. When you have changed the negative emotion, repeat several times so it can't affect you again.

Another reframe can be done if you don't usually get pictures or sounds, but experience negative feelings. This is similar to moving the voice in the chapter 'The Inner Critic':

○ *Where is the feeling? Move it to your thumb, or big toe.*

○ *Does it have a shape? Change the shape.*

○ *What texture does it have? Change that.*

○ *What temperature has it? Make it cold or warm.*

○ *Change any element until all the negative feeling is eliminated.*

Whenever you realise that you have made a negative statement, restate what you said into a positive one by beginning the sentence with 'in the past'. So, 'I'm always lbw against left-armers' can now become 'In the past I used to be lbw by left-armers.'

Reframing can transform you, bring hope from hopelessness, turn despair into delight, build success from apathy. As with everything taught here, you have to practise, then practise some more, but once you know it, you have it for life.

New Thinking = Better Thinking = Better Ability = Better You.

Look at any setback as an opportunity for a comeback. Change your thinking, change your cricket. Go for the change, don't be afraid.

Reframing can be helped by anchoring…

ANCHORING

Don't find fault, find a remedy.

Henry Ford

Remember how you can use the Circle of Excellence to bring about a resourceful state – so it is with anchoring. It's like having a push button to feel excellence.

Anchors exist all around you. Have you come across an old photo which created a pang of emotion? Heard an old song which was popular during a special time of your life? Smelt a particular aroma that brought memories rushing back? Do you frequently visit a location and always sit at the same place? Hold a new-born baby and notice how your emotional state changes.

All these associations trigger memories that take us back to a past experience. They are called 'anchors', as they anchor you to a certain state. The clever thing is you can use these anchors to bring back the whole experience.

The theory behind using what is known as a 'resource anchor' is that if you constantly link the mood or emotion you desire to be in with a meaningful feeling, picture, sound or even taste or smell, you can reproduce that desired mood or emotion when you need it.

This following process, which sets up a resource anchor, only takes a few minutes. Read the routine a couple of times to get it clear in your mind. Now, think of the resourceful state you would like to be in, only choose one resourceful state at a time.

Create a physical signal which you are going to use. What you read in many NLP books is to touch your thumb and forefinger together, but it can be anything you think is appropriate – patting down your hair, scratching an imaginary itch, clasping your hands, rubbing a wrist, crossing your fingers. These are all examples of physical signals; however saying a certain phrase or mantra may do the trick for some people, or looking at something, perhaps the sight screen. It's up to you.

Now, vividly think of a time when you had the ability or emotion you want to repeat. Rewind the clock and add as much detail as you can, remember, see what you saw, hear what you heard, feel how you felt then. Now see, hear, feel all even more fully, experience it intensely. Let it all come back to you, let it build up so you relive it in your whole body. If you can't remember a time, imagine how you would feel if you had that resource. Maybe you have not experienced it in a cricket context before; that's okay, think of any time it has happened and use that.

As the good, remembered experience returns and begins to build up in you to a peak, apply the physical signal, sink into the feeling of being there. Again make it brighter, richer, turn up the volume. The peak when you are in the right state lasts on average between five and fifteen seconds, but for some individuals it could be two seconds, while with a few others, almost a minute.

Now think about an unrelated topic (in NLP jargon this is called 'breaking state'). Do something like remembering a friend's telephone number, saying your name backwards, or reciting a nursery rhyme. This is a distraction, so when you repeat this technique, it's like doing it afresh.

Now repeat four or five times.

When you decide that the resource anchor is functional, break state for the last time. Test to see if the anchor works. Think of something else. Then fire your anchor. You should get back into the resourceful state. If not, apply the stimulus several more times and test again.

If you are having trouble, there are usually a couple of things going on. Make sure you are actually reliving the whole event rather than just thinking about it. You must feel the positive emotion – after all, emotions are energy in action. Have one specific resource or event in mind rather than getting confused by juggling several. Do you understand the process fully? If not, go over it again.

It gets better. Whenever you are experiencing that resource in your normal life, anchor it with the same stimulus you devised so you are 'topping up'.

The great thing with using anchors is they work automatically. Think about a forthcoming event when you or one of your players is feeling anxious and you want to look forward to the game, you can create the resources of concentration, confidence, excitement or relaxation. Imagine everything going perfectly. Picture it in your mind, seeing, hearing, feeling yourself in this good state at that future time. Now fire your anchor.

Do it when you are in different positions or environments. Go to different locations and practise getting yourself into positive moods.

You can look back with satisfaction to see how much further you have developed.

You can create very resourceful states for yourself or your players. If working with someone, it's ideal for you to also be in the same resourceful state as your player wants to be. If any states or emotions your player wants seem to conflict, like being motivated but relaxed, ask the player if they feel they can be in both states at the same time. If they believe they can, all well and good. If not, it's best to create two different anchors – one for motivation and another for relaxation – which you apply separately.

You see how you can become anchored to certain states – unfortunately you may even have created unresourceful states for yourself in the past. What about playing at a ground with negative associations for you or against a player who has had the better of you in the past and makes you feel negative and powerless? We all have negative anchors but the good news is they can be disconnected by a process called 'collapsing anchors'.

Ensure you understand the method fully and you feel comfortable with it. Unless you're a coach applying this with one of your players, it's best to have someone go through this process with you as you may need help to fix the anchors in place. Agree fully that the negative state is to be collapsed and decide what resourceful state is going to replace it. Make sure you are replacing a negative state with a very strong, positive one.

Decide where on your body you are going to apply the resource and remove the negative state. To keep things simple, you would apply the resource stimuli to one side of your body, be it the right knuckles, right shoulder, right knee, and remove the negative state from the opposite left knuckle, left shoulder or left knee.

On a scale of zero to ten how do you feel about the situation?

Remember, if working with a player, have them fully relive the event intensely and as the good feeling peaks they should give you a pre-arranged signal, a nod of the head for example, so you can then anchor the positive resource in position.

Access fully a positive state or memory you or your player have experienced; let's go for competence and anchor that to the right knee as an example. Do this several times, then test to ensure the anchor works.

Break state by thinking about something else. This is important.

Now, once only, remember an unwanted state or memory, for example let's say 'apprehensive'. Relive it and when you or your player feel the emotion, anchor it onto the opposite side of the body, in this case, the left knee.

Break state again by thinking of something else.

Here's the good part. Fire both anchors simultaneously. Continue holding the positive anchor (right knee) for about five seconds after releasing the negative . As long as the resourceful states anchor is stronger than the undesired states, the undesired anchor will collapse and the unresourceful state will no longer affect you. If you picked a strong negative memory, you may need more resources to make the situation more satisfying.

Test by asking yourself or your cricketer how they now feel about the issue on the scale of zero to ten. Has it gone down?

Future-pace by imagining some time in the future when you or they would confront that issue again and notice the response. If the problem has gone, continue imagining the old problem at a number of events in weeks, months or even a year or two into the future until you are certain the problem has gone.

Next is a method to overcome internal conflict…

INTERNAL CONFLICT

Failure is an attitude, not an outcome.

Harvey Mackay

You're the batsman standing alone at the wicket. There's a paradox, as one part of you may have the confidence to take on everything, while another part of you may want to be cautious, as it will keep the wicket safe. A tug-of-war between ambition and performance anxiety. Two conflicting beliefs you have for the same situation will only hold you back. If you are indecisive in your mind, how is your body going to know what to do?

If two incompatible states occur at the same time, you can modify each and reform them into a third state, which is an integration of the original two.

Throughout this book, you have been learning methods which will get your mind working. Some may seem silly, others uncomfortable. Some may challenge your way of thinking, change does that. Take it as a good sign – it's not for the faint-hearted.

This process can cause changes.

Taking the example of two conflicting beliefs above, find a quiet place where you're not going to be disturbed, and get yourself relaxed. Think about the situation causing internal conflict.

Place your hands in front of you, palms up. Imagine the confident part in your dominant hand. See it as a colour, shape, a person, anything to make it real for you.

Do the same with your other hand, where you place your cautious part.

Ask the confident hand what its positive intention is for you. Continue asking until you get the feeling of an answer, even if you think you're imagining it.

Now ask the cautious hand what its positive intention is for you.

Keep asking until you recognise, on some level, that they both want the same outcome. Go through the process even if you think your imagination is playing tricks – it's not.

This is for reference:

○ *Confident Part = more courage = perform better = success*

○ *Cautious Part = anxious = safety = success*

Now imagine that a Successful Part is there between your hands, possessing the resources of confidence and caution.

Slowly bring your hands together until those two separate parts become an integrated whole.

Bring your joined hands up to your chest and imagine you're allowing the new integrated part to step inside you. Convinced?

Next is a slightly different and quicker method to change a negative response into a positive.

Bring to mind a problem or bad memory you have. What would its solution or opposite be where you want a desirable outcome?

Place your non-dominant hand about eighteen inches in front of your face and project your problem onto it. Have your dominant hand behind your back.

Practise by changing hands so your dominant hand is before your face, the other behind your back. Now project the solution onto your dominant hand.

Now you know the movement, get set up as before with the 'problem hand' before your face and as fast as you can, change hands. You can even use a motivational word as you change.

Break state by shaking your hands off, repeating your telephone number, or use some other distraction.

Repeat ten times. You should neutralise the problem and replace it with a beneficial condition.

As you practise this it gets easier to resolve any internal conflict. You can hold on to your seat as you're entering the world where there are no limitations.

Let's talk about motivation…

MOTIVATION

You just can't beat a person who never gives up.

Babe Ruth

'Motivation' is a much-used word in sport. It comes from the Latin word meaning 'to move'. The most important thing for you however is to love your cricket.

Most people can access unhappiness, guilt, even depression quite easily. By thinking of some failure in your life you open up undesirable emotions. The opposite can be the same. You can feel confident, excited, happy, you don't have to have a reason!

When you have played well, you can repeat it by accessing the same levels of arousal that you experienced at that good time.

Here are some methods to increase motivation:

Change livens things up; can you vary your training routine, different exercise, new place?

Decreasing your rate of breathing will affect your nervous system. Slow, deep breathing through your nose creates relaxation in body and mind.

Someone could call the nervous energy before a game 'anxiety', you could label it 'excitement'. Rename nervousness, boredom, drudgery to something more inspiring. How does 'another type of excitement' sound, or 'adventure'?

Release any tense, nervous energy by moving the muscles before any game. Tense and relax each muscle group. You should do this during a warm-up anyway. A fielder can shift from foot to foot to sway into a calm, relaxed state of awareness.

Use key words that can excite or inspire you. 'Easy', 'power', 'winner', even your name or team name. Create words or phrases that are personal but powerful for you.

Use upbeat music to arouse you. On the pitch, play it in your head.

Suppose you have a boring task ahead of you. Picture something that motivates you, then trick yourself into changing the chore so it looks and feels exactly the same as the one that gets you going. As you've learnt, altering the variables, brightness, colour, position, shape, size, sound, can change how you react.

These are the steps:

Remember something that pleased you, a triumph you would wish to experience again. Maybe the result of your last over. Concentrate on that image while you ask yourself:

o   *Is it a still picture or a movie?*

o   *Is it in colour or black and white?*

o   *Is it close to you or further away?*

o *What size?*

o *Are you inside it, like it's wrapped around you, or outside and you're looking in?*

o *If any movement, is it fast or slow?*

o *If the image is in front of you, are you looking from above or below it?*

Look at the boring task you want to feel motivated about. Ask yourself the same questions and notice what's different or the same about the two pictures.

Move the unmotivated picture into the space occupied by the triumphant picture. Change everything to make it look and feel the same as the triumphant picture.

Intensify it, make it vibrant. Give it more of what you've given it. Hear the band playing a theme tune. Even imagine pressure on your back as if someone was pushing you into the picture. Make it real.

Do this change quickly, forcefully. Do it five times, breaking the state between each change, so that you're starting as new each time.

By telling your brain to represent the tedious picture in this exciting new way, the happy changes you make tell your brain: 'I don't want this… I want this.' So, how do you feel about the boring task? It should feel better, more achievable.

As I mentioned in another chapter, use language carefully. Words and phrases represent something, they are like symbols. Your words literally can become your world. Complete these positive statements:

- ○ *I am in the process of...*

- ○ *I've decided...*

- ○ *It excites me when...*

Let's investigate the power of mirroring...

MIRRORING

A champion is afraid of losing, everyone else is afraid of winning.

Billie Jean King

Anything practised continually over time becomes an automatic behaviour. Problems arise when the practice is not perfect. If it's not spot-on, the cricketer creates a varied pathway to the required standard, resulting in poor performance.

Even as an adult, you can still find a place for role models who represent and support the standards you embrace, and you should never outgrow your need for this type of hero who can be an inspiration to you.

If you're new to cricket, or about to take on an unfamiliar role – wicket keeper for example – you have nothing to use as a reference to achieving a particular level. Do the same things in the same way as someone who has excelled at it. Do the same things in the same way as someone who has done it successfully.

Choose a skill you would like to master. Imagine what having that ability can do for you. If you can, remember having done the skill in the past to the level you want.

Choose a role model, someone you respect and admire, who easily exhibits that skill. Someone who has walked that road. Get yourself a DVD if you are able. Watch out for the subtle information, study their hands and notice how they move their wrists, notice where they are looking. You will be amazed what you pick up and it's a great mental exercise in observation.

Become a director and make a movie in your mind of your hero demonstrating that skill effortlessly. Press Play and watch carefully your hero doing everything perfectly from beginning to end. Watch out for any distinctions you need to note.

Observe how your role model carries her/himself. How do they move? Imagine how they talk to themselves positively.

Play the movie again, this time including yourself beside or behind your role model, imitating their actions, breathing, voice, mimic everything exactly.

Now climb in and disguise yourself as your hero, synchronise fully. Modify everything until the animation is exactly as you wish. See through their eyes, hear through their ears, take on the feelings of how empowered s/he is.

Feel what it's like to be your role model having that skill. Build up the feelings, sounds, sights. See all around you how other people respond.

How different does your future look? How much more optimism do you have as a result of this perfect skill? Live this future, make it real for yourself.

Step out and away and imagine in front of you the other you who now exhibits the skills, assurance, energy you have made your own. Make any modifications.

If your role model has written instructions in a book or manual, or had themselves filmed, get a copy to study. Do research. Find out what the person did to find success. Understand how they think.

Continue to rehearse until you are certain you can perform their skill automatically. Even if you feel like you're making it up, you're teaching your brain a new behaviour, so pretend until it becomes natural.

Remember the different scenarios your hero has played in. How did your hero deal with any unforeseen challenges and problems that happened before, during and after the game?

A further technique like this is 'modelling'. Here you should also choose the right role models and use their examples to inspire you and change any past, unproductive beliefs, behaviours, limitations or doubts – you don't have any!

Study a group of players in your favoured position, as by observing a group it allows you to identify what it is that is essential to them all, mixed in with what qualities are unique to each individual. You can then personalise and develop what is uniquely yours.

It is a valid thought that modelling can oversimplify the topic of achieving success as it does not take into consideration natural talent or social upbringing. An example would be your physical condition and social attributes. You may never have the potential to become an international wicket keeper. However, if you were to examine the world's greatest wicket keepers, you would possibly find patterns in their diets, lifestyles, training and mindset. Duplicating these patterns is not a guarantee you will duplicate their skill level, but it will guarantee you will become as good a wicket keeper as you can be, given your genetic potential.

When mirroring or modelling a great player, you will never step into their footsteps, I'm sorry to say; what you will do though is leave your own tracks. Anything is possible and they will be your own tracks. Pretend you're an exceptional cricketer, act as if it were true and soon your mind will forget to pretend, and you will have mastered it.

Feeling good? Want to create happiness on demand?

You can with the inner smile…

THE INNER SMILE

There's more ways of getting out than is shown in t'rules.
Wilfred Rhodes

When you're happy your body creates a chemical, serotonin, known as the 'happy chemical'. It releases tension, controls pain, gives your immune system a boost and promotes wellbeing throughout your body.

Remember times when you were happy and light-hearted. If you can't think of a particular time, how about a comedy show or film, even jokes you've heard. Go over them while you turn up the brightness, the colour, the sounds, make them richer, remember how good you felt until you find yourself smiling with pure joy. Double that feeling. Do it again. How do you feel?

Imagine now how much better your life could be if you were like this all the time. Happiness plays an important role in your success. Imagine in your mind's eye when you have read this chapter feeling good, feeling refreshed.

Vividly imagine your eyes smiling, a glint in them dancing there. Raise the corners of your mouth as if you have a special secret.

106

Get a sense of where that feeling is strongest. Play with it some more. Increase it, give it a happy colour and roll it up to the top of your head and down to the bottom of your feet. Imagine every cell glowing with delight.

You can do this anywhere. Doing something you once found difficult proves itself to be relatively easy. It's good to imagine all the benefits this is going to give you, isn't it?

Put a smile anywhere in your body that feels uncomfortable or tense. When you think about relationships, training, games, smile with the same energy and notice your mood begin to lift.

Here's a bonus. These happy chemicals create more connections in the brain every time you have a pleasant experience. So not only can your body experience happiness, the more often it happens, the more intelligent you become. What was a technique has now become a positive attitude.

And you can be more positive with relationships...

RELATIONSHIPS

It's a funny kind of month, October. For the really keen
cricket fan it's when you realise your wife left you in May.
Denis Norden

This chapter is about people you know who are involved in cricket.

You know what the atmosphere is like, talking to each other after a game and hearing the peal of distant church bells, seeing the plumpness of the home-made cakes. As the sun goes down, comradeship in the local tavern or barbeque goes up with the laughter from all the banter and those catching excuses.

A side full of talent is great to have, but you can also have a team that is greater than the sum of its parts. As long as you have support in your changing room, that's all that matters. Bring problems or troubles into the open as soon as possible. If too much gets swept under the carpet, the carpet begins to smell.

Cricket can be a very competitive environment and some 'powers' sometimes like to play one off against the other. We do get some who emphatically are not nice. Selfishness and jealousy motivate some people. If you are stuck with someone like that in your team, smile and think of it as punishment for everything you put your mum and dad through when you were younger!

Often it's not the opposition that can be a barrier, but family, friends, work colleagues or team-mates who are the problem. 'You'll never be good enough' or 'Don't set your sights too high'. As well-meaning as they think they are, it's easier to make an ambitious player worse than better. If you take notice of people who tell you what you can't do, you will never accomplish anything. You're placed in a negative frame of mind, have a conflict of priorities and it all spills over into a poor sporting performance.

You often get hostile, intolerant coaches who think they're being helpful by criticising you. Some players respond well to sarcasm, but not all. 'You'll never be a batsman' does not work for everyone. Often you go onto the pitch and make mistakes because a negative expectation has been set up in your mind.

Likewise, if a new coach shouts at you when you're in the nets, often you can place more meaning into the episode than is intended. You begin to feel anger, frustration or humiliation as you think the insensitive coach has no respect for you or does not like you. What else could that shouting mean? It does not mean they disapprove of you. The coach may be showing passion, enthusiasm or perhaps it's his/her way of pushing you further, knowing you have potential to do better.

Get to understand one another's point of view. Have compassion to understand and sympathise with others by putting yourself in their shoes. Be aware that negativity can rub off on those around you. Is it good to put others through your disappointments?

Have you had an argument with someone, maybe the captain and hours later you're still reliving it, still seeing the captain's face and hearing the words? If you change the picture and sounds as described in the chapter 'Imagination', you can change your feelings.

What about a conflict of ideas with a coach, official or team-mate? Suppose you have been rested. A lot will go on inside your head. Rationalise first. How are your stats? Perhaps you should consider what they have said before dismissing it. The truth can hurt sometimes, but putting yourself in others' shoes makes you adaptable so can give you further insight:

Go to a time when you had a difference of opinion with someone. Visualise that person stood before you now, notice all the detail.

Now step out of your body and let any emotions go. This will soon start to make sense.

Step into their body and notice the world from their perspective, seeing, hearing, feeling and thinking from their point of view.

Next, step away from their body and let their feelings go.

Think of someone you admire. A friend, hero, even a character from the past who is mature, intelligent and wise. Step into their body and see that person considering you and your foe from a neutral position.

Are there any insights you can find? What advice would this mentor give you?

Lastly, step back into your own body, taking with you anything you have learned. Can you move toward a resolution? Do you see things differently?

Most cricketers don't get to play for the Ashes. Follow your goals and not the crowd. You may feel envious when your friends go to parties, often the parties aren't that much anyway. You can make up for it later. Avoid people and distractions that can turn you away from your dreams. Sometimes you may have to let go of old friendships if a fire to succeed in cricket burns in you.

Almost every day, the sport pages print embarrassing and sometimes tragic stories of car crashes, drunken behaviour, drug suspensions, gambling. Lives and careers have been ruined by the poor choices some sportspeople have made. There is always somebody ready with a camera. There seems to be a saying with some of the tabloids: 'Don't let the facts get in the way of a good story.' People who are easily recognised, in the public eye, have a responsibility toward furthering the traditional qualities of cricket and making sure it is presented in a good image.

One of the best ways to improve is to mix with successful, skilful people. Surround yourself with achievers who provide good teaching and will make you better. Find a few people, cricketers, umpires, sport journalists, anyone who understands the game. Invite them out for a drink or a meal. Be cheeky, write to them for advice. Let them know you want to pick their brains on how you can be a success. They become aware of you and understand you are serious. Be humble. Listen. As long as you're respectful, most people will enjoy the opportunity to help you. Other people can also see situations without the emotional baggage you may carry.

Take advantage of the experience of coaches and senior players; they have lived the challenges you face and know how to deal with them, or they have failed so you can learn from their mistakes. Ask those involved in the game to tell you what advice they would give another player on how to beat you. What are your strong points and weak ones? In what ways do they see you're vulnerable?

Ask a favourite player in your team his keys to performance success. What are they doing when they are really on their game?

How do they do those things? Now what I want you to do before a game is focus on their answers.

A key to reaching your potential is learning to listen to others. Lean toward them when they speak. Place your tongue on the roof of your mouth; this quietens internal dialogue so you can pay attention to the other person. Don't interrupt or finish others' sentences. People will appreciate your listening skills. If someone interrupts while you're speaking, politely ask them to wait until you have finished, then listen while they speak.

Praise others also. Being critical, judgemental or opinionated are three ways to see relationships disappear. Use integrity. Impart sound knowledge and experience to junior players, set an example. Chat about the game all the time, develop their team spirit as well as guide them to be better players.

We all get grumpy and out of sorts occasionally, so when you show up for training excited and pumped up and find one of your team-mates in a far less happy frame than you, find out if they will tell you what's up. 'Is there anything I can do?' may be all that's needed for them to divulge their trials and upsets. Most people having a tough time are not looking for a fight. Once they know you are willing to be supportive, you will be appreciated.

Excitement and passion are contagious. Don't allow others to put you off, or pull you down. And remember, scientists proved bumblebees couldn't fly. But the scientists didn't tell the bumblebees. You have more potential than you or others realise.

Let's look at the interesting subject of time management…

TIME MANAGEMENT

Put your hand on a hot stove for a minute, it seems like an hour. Sit with a pretty girl for an hour, it seems like a minute.

Albert Einstein

Most of us find it difficult to live in the present, we think about past experiences and worry about future ones. Time passes at different rates for each of us. Your unconscious mind doesn't compare time passing the same as your conscious mind, which does so by a clock, watch or other timepiece.

Time varies depending on the circumstances you find yourself in. When you're nervous, in pain, or sad, time slows down. The clock seems to drag – a couple of minutes are like half an hour – or even stands still.

Long boring periods waiting to go out to bat can cause the batsman to lose concentration and sharpness. For any position, test cricket can be a long game.

In contrast, when you're excited and happy, maybe having a great game, the time flashes by.

You can manipulate time if you imagine a situation and slow the process right down to practise and improve a skill. Teach your body to do the right things instinctively by training your mind to pass on the information more quickly. I'll show you. Let's take your style of bowling.

The art of spin bowling can be more mentally challenging than pace or seam so get yourself into a relaxed state. If you're better closing your eyes, do so. Hold a real ball in your hand. If you can't, pretend you have one. Feel its weight, the coolness. Notice the stitching at the seam, the smell of it.

Carefully examine the correct movements of spin bowling. Feel for yourself the whole process of delivery, go through each step so you can physically remember the movements of grip, arm, shoulder, don't forget the run-up involving hips, legs, feet.

See each element in slow motion, at a snail's pace. Go over them several times, making sure that the feel of each element is right. When you're happy, speed it all up. Imagine yourself bowling as you would for real. Feel mighty, make everything colourful, vivid, see the batsman, despondent as you intimidate him. See him successfully bowled out, the ball smashing through the stumps.

What if you're the guardian of the wickets? Do the same only this time feel the bat in your hands. Smell the oiled willow, bring in every sense while you stand comfortable, feeling more and more relaxed, you have plenty of time. Again start in slow motion so your technique is correct, then speed up for real time. You are more prepared to face a fast bowler and score runs by avoiding risk. As you focus on the frustrated bowler, see the hundred-miles-per-hour ball coming toward you at a slow rate. Hear the sweet spot connect as you send the ball rocketing.

With every mental rehearsal, detail will increase. The practice you can make in your mind in a few minutes would require hours of practice in real time. Your unconscious can't tell the difference between what's real and what's imagined, which is why this technique is perfect if you're out through injury. It can help keep you focused.

Want to know how to get the ball to slow down? As the bowler is walking back to his mark before delivering another ball, look up and down the wicket and imagine it is longer than twenty-two yards, so the bowler seems further away than he is. This may help convince you that the ball cannot come at you so fast as it now has further to travel. Practise this in the nets first before attempting it during a match.

Enjoy the activity as you see yourself perform at your best. And give yourself positive suggestions.

Here's an easy activity to help you place cricket as your number one daily priority. Get yourself a calendar, diary or inexpensive day planner. If it pictures cricket so much the better. Start your day with it by writing down the time you plan to train, play competitively or read a motivational book or magazine, then plan the rest of your day around that event, no matter what. Make this a daily commitment. You have made cricket your top priority and arrange everything else around it rather than 'trying to fit cricket in'.

In the next chapter you're going to learn to conquer fear…

FEAR

(False Evidence Appearing Real)

It's not a question of getting rid of butterflies, it's a question of getting them to fly in formation.

John Donohue

The reason for a lot of underachievement in sport is fear. You may have set targets, then done little or nothing to go after them. You worry or get frustrated over your performance, confusion sets in and positive thinking just doesn't help.

We all have a primitive fight-or-flight response built into us for survival. This response will be explained more fully in the 'Pain Control' chapter. We either fight or flee from whatever is threatening us. Today, most of our dangers are not a threat to life and limb, but a psychological threat to our self-esteem and ego.

What I'm going to discuss here is not a sporting technique itself; however some players go through anxieties during their cricket careers. You're uneasy in lifts, you're afraid of cats, dogs, birds. You don't like flying and your team is off to a foreign location. Worrying about your most intimidating opponent, whom you soon have to face, makes your stomach tremble. As you can see, fear creates limitations for you and can turn into a phobia.

Nobody is born with a fear or a phobia. Many phobias can be traced back to an unpleasant incident when a person was younger. Their elder brother may have locked them in a cupboard when they were a young child. What if the dark cupboard was full of moths, or even spiders! Since then, whenever they see moths or spiders or they are in an enclosed space, they relive the event.

The fear of failure prevents people from reaching their full potential. Fear of failure prevents more cricketers from succeeding than any opponent. Fear actually creates the situations that stop cricketers from winning. A paradox of sport is that fear of failure actually makes failure more likely. You bat defensively after the ball snaps up at your ribcage when intuition tells you to go on the offensive. You're afraid of losing, of making mistakes.

Some people are just as afraid of winning! They hear they are shortlisted for a higher team and their world collapses! The thought of the consequences inhibits them. Those with a low opinion of themselves or their ability become uncomfortable around success.

Here's an example. If a talented professional cricketer is frightened to death of public speaking, they could sabotage their success to avoid press interviews. The problem is something not directly related to playing cricket, but will certainly inhibit success.

I repeat: fear of failure actually makes failure more likely. The Law of Dominant Thought states that focusing on something increases the likelihood that it will happen. If you're worried you are going to play badly in a cup game for some reason, guess how you will play? Fear makes you play safe. Fear makes you play small.

An injury can create a fear response as you may be scared of hurting yourself again, then suffering through the agony of more recovery time. There can be a lot of adrenaline pumping around when you start playing again. It can be difficult getting your mind around a comeback after suffering a broken bone; perhaps as a fielder you may hesitate about diving in the gully for a passing ball after you damaged your collar bone a previous time.

Look at it this way, a fear, even a phobia, is an overcompensating protection mechanism. You didn't learn it, you over-learned it and the good news is because it was learned, it can be unlearned.

Morning, noon and night as a batsman you are under siege. Your subconscious raises its head when you feel overwhelmed in this way, warning you to be cautious, anxious, fearful. Now some lucky people can experience these feelings as excitement. But you may be nervous about the bounce, length, deviation or pace of a delivery as you go out to bat and that feeling starts.

Acknowledge your unconscious, thank it for the warning, it's done its job, now let it go. You don't need its presence, now switch your focus to getting on with the job at hand and take care of what you need to concentrate on. Concentration is a good antidote for anxiety.

This following technique is known in NLP as the 'Fast Phobia Cure' or the 'Movie Theatre' technique:

Let's say you have developed a bowling problem: you now expect your front foot to land beyond the crease, causing you to deliver too many wide balls – trepidation of pie-chuckers has set in.

Close your eyes and get yourself comfortable. Give this your full involvement. Imagine you're sitting in a cinema, you can remember a real one if you wish. The screen is blank. You're in charge of the remote control there in your hand.

On a scale of zero to ten, zero being nothing, ten being severe, what number is the problem you're having?

In a moment you're going to play a movie of yourself and the problem you have. As it's a past event, the movie has aged, so it's poor quality and the colour has faded, even turned sepia. You will play your movie in a rectangle in the centre of the screen, not all of the screen.

Compose a comical theme tune, something like The Muppets, Monty Python, Popeye or similar.

Before you press Play, remember a time when you know you were confident and excited about bowling. Feel all that good energy and let it spread all around your body. Now intensify it. Turn up the volume. Maintain that good feeling while you watch the movie. You may even use anchoring to create a resourceful state if the fear you're facing should get out of hand.

Now pay attention. Behind you is the projection booth. To get further distance from your fear, imagine yourself leaving your body sat there in the chair and floating up toward the projection booth. From here, you can observe yourself watching the movie, watching yourself.

You will play the film of your bad event from beginning to end, where it will then freeze-frame. Go ahead and press Play on the remote.

When the film reaches that last frame press Stop. Now watch yourself in the cinema seat rise and go up there to the still picture and congratulate the younger you for being so brave for going through and surviving that nasty experience. It's as if you see yourself from the spectators' perspective, or your coach's. Up in the projection booth the real you is safe. With that acknowledgement watch yourself return to your seat.

When you're ready, run the whole film backwards at top speed, hearing that comical music play. Then play the movie forwards then backwards at fast speed several times. How do you feel? Is there a difference to the memory? On a scale of zero to ten, where is it now? Has the old response gone? If so float back down to your seat and, feeling fully whole again, rise and exit the cinema.

We all get anxious but people plagued by fear get anxious about being anxious. Accept fear and recognise it as the body's way of telling you to become energised. Control the adrenaline, you can then face any difficulty and come out smiling.

Or try 'spinning'…

SPINNING

Life's too short to be afraid.

Robbie Williams

This is a simple, quick-fix technique taught by Paul McKenna, whom I acknowledge here for it. You may find it interesting. It's ideal when you find yourself in a shaky or stressful situation which needs to be addressed there and then. The concept is that all feelings start in one place within your body and move in a prescribed direction, so by reversing the direction of the bad feeling, you can eliminate it.

Go through this routine while thinking about your problem – say, poor ability to judge the length and bounce from a very fast bowler. On a scale of zero to ten, zero being nothing and ten being extremely uncomfortable, where are you at the moment?

Think about what's disturbing you and get an idea of where that feeling begins. Usually it's around the stomach/solar plexus and moves upward toward your throat.

Imagine lifting that feeling out of your body and watching it spin before you like a wheel.

Imagine what colour it is. Now change that colour to your favourite.

Maybe imagine a pleasant noise or music.

With a flip, turn the wheel upside down so that it spins in the opposite direction.

When you feel calmer about the situation, pull the wheel back into your body to where it started, still spinning in the opposite direction.

Let it speed up, faster and faster, until the anxiety or upset begins to fade away and finally disappear. On the scale of zero to ten, where do you find the problem now? You may now be able to build up your innings. Problems can vanish entirely.

You can also replace an undesirable state with a desirable one using 'swish'…

SWISH

This strategy can bring freedom from self-doubt, maybe the dread of dropping a catch which is on its way toward you. The trick is to have your positive image on the catapult in its high-tension position ready to fire so that your mind accepts the image as going one way – toward you.

First, place in front of you a picture of an image you would like of yourself, assertive, powerful, something that can give you goose bumps of excitement. Something that is realistic and attainable. Make it exciting. Have it full of the skills or qualities you would like more of, a natural catcher, a stroke master. Make the details vivid, see yourself oozing with confidence, then make it larger, the colours bright, add sparkle, play a theme tune that's upbeat, adding vitality. Add the approving voices of coaches or team-mates. Make everything rich and intense. I really want you to live in this so include anything that improves the image.

Imagine this picture of your image has thick rubber bands attached to each corner which are fixed to a firing mechanism next to you. The picture is slowly pulled away from you, stretching off into the distance on those rubber bands, so that it seems like a giant catapult is being aimed at you ready to fire. Lock that exciting picture in place and be aware of the tension in those stretched rubber bands. Your hands are on the firing lever.

Now bring up a second image of a memory of whatever it is that's giving you a lack of confidence, fear, inertia, under-performance, where you would benefit from a new self-image. Let's say slow hands behind the wicket. Drain away any colour, turn down the focus, shrink it down, quieten any sound.

Before you fire the first, good image, think of a motivational word to use as you fire the catapult. Originally it used to be 'swish' as that is how therapists had the two images interchanged, but any word appropriate to you or the situation can be more effective.

When you're ready, feel yourself fire the catapult so that the exciting image shoots up right in front of you, its acceleration tearing through that poor second image or memory, so you end with that exciting first picture before you. If it's done fast enough, you may even jump. Don't forget to add the inspiring word.

Notice any changes to how you feel. Reset the positive image by stretching back the elastic band again under tension so you have before you the remnants of a broken second image of what had made you feel bad. With that poor picture in front of you, fire again so that the good one once again rips through the bad, blasting through it once more.

Do this five times. Each time that first positive image shoots toward you, it ends bigger and brighter and louder, while the poor second image is gradually reduced to shreds until the last time, when it is completely destroyed.

Another technique to reduce or eliminate problems is 'tapping'…

TAPPING

Human feelings are words expressed in human flesh.

Aristotle

Meridian energy systems have been demonstrated often by Paul McKenna on TV. The premise is that when you experience a negative emotional upset, you experience an energetic imbalance in your body's energy system and by correcting that imbalance, you can go on to heal any emotional or physical issues.

It's fast, safe and easy to do, having an overwhelming amount of evidence proving it works. It was created by Dr Roger Callahan, a psychologist trained in acupuncture, applied kinesiology and NLP. He devised TFT (thought field therapy) from insights with his knowledge from these three fields, as a psychological version of acupuncture. It tends to use a lot of acupuncture points which are very specific and applied in a certain sequence.

Gary Craig, a master practitioner of NLP, is the founder of EFT (emotional freedom technique). He took TFT and distilled it into a simpler version, which is much more widely used and accessible for anyone to learn. Using a simple, painless procedure you tap on the same acupuncture points on your body so as you tap in the prescribed sequence, you distract your mind to reduce the unpleasant experience.

Other systems have followed which all deal with an imbalance in the energy system – TAT, BSFF, Emotrance – and some have modified EFT.

All these procedures seem to access the meridian energy system where any emotions become trapped. The tapping creates vibrations in the energy system which appear to release the original energy disturbance and restore the even flow, somewhat like tapping on your central heating pipes to clear an airlock.

Unconvinced? Like many of the techniques in this manual, it seems strange at first, so is controversial, but it is based on scientific fact and has produced quick and substantial changes for many. For convenience, I will use the version demonstrated by Paul McKenna on TV and in his publications.

This process can reduce or eliminate any strong, defeatist feelings, beliefs, memories, emotions, and it can also reduce physical symptoms.

While tapping, you must continue thinking about your problem throughout the whole sequence.

Close your eyes and think about your problem. Let's say you always play poorly on a slow, cracked pitch. You have painful accounts of unpredictable bounce and ducking short balls coming at your ribs. On a scale of zero to ten, zero being nothing and ten being the worst it could ever be, where is your problem?

Still thinking about the problem pitch, take two fingers of either hand and tap firmly ten times above one of your eyebrows.

Now tap under that eye ten times.

Now tap ten times under your collar bone.

As you continue to think about your problem, tap under your armpit ten times.

Tap on the 'karate chop' side of your other hand.

Tap on the back of your other hand between the knuckles of your ring finger and little finger.

Open your eyes, then close them. Keep tapping. The following eye movements are connected to various brain functions.

Open your eyes. Look down to your right, then centre, then down to your left.

Keep tapping and as you do so, rotate your eyes 360 degrees anti-clockwise, then 360 degrees clockwise.

Still thinking about the slow pitch, hum the first few lines of 'Happy Birthday' or a favourite tune. This humming allows switching between right brain hemisphere – left brain hemisphere – right brain hemisphere activity.

Next count aloud from one to five.

Repeat the first few lines of 'Happy Birthday' or your favourite tune.

Still thinking on the problem, close your eyes, tap ten times above your eye again.

Again tap under your collar bone.

Tap under your armpit.

Finally tap on the 'karate chop' point again.

Where is your problem regarding the slow pitch now on the scale of zero to ten? You should have it down to a manageable level by the second go. If it hasn't reduced, go over the sequence again. It depends on how strong your problem was to start with, so it may need several attempts to reduce or completely eliminate it. Repeat as needed. You may get confused about what used to bother you.

Next, improve your game arousal with the 'thermometer'…

THERMOMETER

And Ian Gregg's on eight, including two fours.

Jim Laker

As a batsman you need two fields of vision: a wide angle which will take in everything you can see from the crease, how the field is set, the boundaries, the sight screen, crowd movement; while your more narrow view takes in the bowler and the seam of the ball. You need to be at your optimum arousal to give your best, neither too psyched up nor too relaxed.

Here is a practical suggestion to maintain optimum arousal. Get yourself really comfortable and remember a time when your arousal was near perfect and how you felt then. Really get there and relive all those good feelings, sights and sounds. Make them bigger and bolder, more and more vivid.

Imagine a large thermometer with a scale that reads from zero to 200. What colour is the scale? While you are in this perfect state, the reading on the scale will be set to 100. Remember how to set an anchor? Create one now, something easy, like squeezing a wrist.

Now remember a time when your arousal was too high for optimum performance, too psyched up or too angry. Get in touch with any feelings or emotions you had then and imagine the scale reading 160 or 170. To reach your best performance state of 100, breath slowly and gently, say 'relax' or 'calm' and fire your anchor to reach those good feelings. Notice the scale begin to drop down about ten or fifteen points.

Keep taking more relaxed, calm breaths while your anchor is grasped until you reach 100 on the scale. Practise this several times to train yourself to reduce high levels of arousal.

This time remember a time when you had low arousal, too carefree maybe. When you have something imagine the scale is at 30 or 40. Again, breathe deeply and imagine energy coming in, see the scale begin to rise as you release your resource anchor. Repeat several times more as the scale reaches 100.

Rehearse using breathing and remembering all the associations that bring you to 100 on the scale so it becomes automatic; this method will help you achieve regular, frequent performances toward your ideal performance state.

Now I'll show you how the future can be your friend with a time line...

TIME LINE

If my mind can conceive it, and I can believe it, I then can achieve it.

Larry Holmes

Part of you that is curious may wonder about this experience. Think of a time ahead when you can see yourself celebrating a success – how about Player of the Season, or holding aloft a trophy as captain while you celebrate with your team-mates, the champagne corks popping, your supporters cheering. When you imagine that kind of future, your unconscious is directed toward making it happen.

Devised by Tad James, another great psychology pioneer, a time line is explained as an imaginary line where events happen and even where the unconscious stores memories. This line stretches off in one direction to your future and in the opposite direction to your past. Examples of this would be when you say 'I'm looking forward to seeing you' or 'I'll put this problem in the past'.

There are two parts to this exercise. First, how do you represent time? Think about something you do every day, if it's cricket-related so much the better. As you see yourself doing this activity tomorrow, notice the direction you looked. Was your future in front, or was it to your left or right? Higher or lower? How far away?

131

Think about doing that task next week. Is the image further away, in front, behind, to the side? Higher or lower? Stay with me on this. What about a week ago in the past? Where were you doing the activity then?

Think about doing the same thing a month in the future. Is the image closer or further away? More in front or behind, more to one side or another? How about a month ago?

You can go on imagining the same activity three, six, twelve months in the future. Where is the picture?

Imagine all these pictures are dots joined together by a line as if you were connecting the dots inside your mind. This is how you unconsciously see time, your time line.

The second part of this exercise is creating your cricketing future, then live into it. Project yourself several months into your future, maybe the end of a rewarding season, see from your mind's eye out. Or maybe you have reached a goal. Everything has gone well, your game has improved, you're more confident, you're more knowledgeable. You have achievements in your life outside cricket.

Be curious about your future. Form an image of that ideal scene of everything you wish to happen in your future. It can be real or symbolic. See yourself there, happy and successful. Make the image big, bright, bold, richly colourful, and anticipate how good you will feel the sparkle.

Now fill in the steps along the way to this ideal scene. Make a smaller image and place it a few weeks, or months, before this final big picture. Keep doing this until you have a succession of images connecting the present to your ideal future so that they get bigger each time, with good things happening along the way.

Look at those pictures you have created as stepping-stones and imagine floating up out of your body and into each picture, spending a few moments living in each to absorb the positive experiences.

When you reach that final image, really get into the feeling of achievement as you discover yourself already there.

Finally return to the present and look along your future time line. Have confidence in the knowledge that it is a map for your unconscious to bring fulfilment to the future you have created.

Next, let's change your thinking about injury…

INJURIES

Listen son, you haven't broken your leg. It's all in the mind.

Bill Shankly, OBE

Let's suppose you generally field on the boundary. You have pain in your shoulder. Batting and bowling are okay, it's the return throwing that causes the discomfort. But it's still a case of wanting to play and not let the side down even if you have a 'little niggle'. There you are with repetitive strain injury. All that throwing from the boundary has taken its toll.

The trauma from an injury can be more psychological and emotional than the physical damage. The fear of it happening again can be more intense than the injury sustained.

Often psychological features will boost or impede healing. Any change in your physical condition will be accompanied by a change in your mental-emotional state, either consciously or unconsciously, and vice versa. You need to be aware how you respond to an injury which may stop you playing and regularly ask yourself these questions which will affect your rehabilitation and recovery phase:

- *How do I perceive the injury?*

- *How am I personally handling the injury?*

- *What is my emotional response to the injury?*

- *What is my emotional response to others?*

- *How frustrated do I feel?*

- *How frustrated do I feel about not playing?*

- *What is my commitment to recovery?*

- *What is my speed of recovery?*

- *Am I keeping to the rehabilitation programme?*

- *How does the injury affect my goals?*

- *How do my team-mates perceive my injury?*

- *What do I need from my family and friends to help me cope?*

- *What psychological strategies am I using?*

Some of the psychological strategies you can use include changing beliefs, goal setting, healing imagery, performance imagery, positive self-talk, removing fear, relaxation exercise and visualisation which are all described in other chapters. Psychological strategies and mental interventions not only help to enhance successful sporting performance, they also enhance successful recovery.

Run videos in your head of doing well; this keeps your mind focused and positive. Your mind stores what you have experienced and what you have thought the same way. This is perfect for mental training. You can train using visualisation to sharpen good technical and tactical techniques. The advantage is you can go through several repetitions of any technique in minutes without causing further injury.

There are a number of ways you can use the power of your imagination to accelerate recovery of injury; the following chapter, 'Pain Control', will detail three, but here is a brief list which you may wish to consider:

Healing imagery, when you can imagine a light, colour, sensation, even a sound, bathe the injured area so you can almost feel healing taking place.

Performance imagery, when you will recall or re-experience your cricket skills and remember feelings associated with a good performance, or visualise a future event, maybe taking most of the wickets in a game for a low run rate expenditure, not forgetting to add in the good emotions you will have.

Recovery imagery, as you effectively visualise full strength and mobility.

Treatment imagery; here you would be fully engaged during a therapy session, imagining the treatment working effectively and powerfully.

A major requirement for an ambitious cricketer is fitness. Fast bowlers can put a great amount of pressure on their lower backs if they bowl for long periods. They need to improve flexibility to keep supple. It's tough if you find yourself out through injury. You can do nothing, or you can use your time wisely. List the things you can do, see opportunities, perhaps studying DVDs, reading, cheering on your team-mates. Perform any exercises you can do, even if it's sitting on an exercise bike with your arm in a sling.

Psychological and social support is most important to assist recovery, and it is frequently overlooked that others can assist in the recovery process. In the past it was easy to ignore someone who was injured, with the additional attitude that they were letting the side down. Very frustrating for the lonely patient!

It is important that the patient still feels a part of the team and integrates with them frequently during the rehabilitation, along with the coaching staff and medical staff. This is big, as affection, empathy, concern, appropriate feedback information, or just being listened to, enable you to feel better, recover faster and reintegrate with the team and your social network.

Goal-setting is important as it will enable you to develop daily and weekly goals to be used in your journey toward recovery. Included here are the therapy sessions, rehabilitation exercise programme and mental training.

How about an injured opponent? Is it real or exaggerated? Ignore anything they say about their aches and pains. Assume it's for gamesmanship, sympathy or heroics. Give them no attention until after the match. You're a fast bowler – you cannot worry if the batsman gets hurt, it puts too much pressure on you and can ruin your style. If your opponent can stand on the field of play, they are healthy enough to warrant your best efforts. If their injury is real or not, it can have a negative influence on you.

Injured? Let's talk about pain control...

PAIN CONTROL

Around the wicket, umpire, and call an ambulance.

Steve Kirby

You must only use pain-control techniques when you know the cause of the pain. Pain means there is something wrong. If there is something wrong, you must find medical assistance.

No medical claims are expressed or implied here. Whatever the results you get, please continue to take any medication or actions prescribed by your health practitioner.

If you suffer pain or discomfort in any part of your body, just fifteen minutes of this exercise can make it disappear or diminish it significantly. Using the power of their minds, people who performed this during a clinical test were able to reduce pain by up to eighty percent.

A closed-eye process is best, so learn the method first, or have someone read it to you. The purpose of this exercise is to look at the pain from a different perspective so you look beyond the pain. To your surprise you can get rid of it. Want it to happen, expect it to happen, allow it to happen. The power of your mind is enough.

Get yourself relaxed somewhere you won't be disturbed. Without being cynical, without judging if you are doing it right, dismiss your rational mind and locate specifically the condition you're suffering. Now describe it.

How big is it? How long, thick, wide? What shape is it? A cube, flat, rectangle, round, square, triangle, is it jagged? Is it dull or sharp?

Just keep focusing on the condition. Describe exactly what it feels like. Pounding, pressing, pulsating, stretching, tearing?

Does it have a colour? A smell? A weight? If you're not sure, just make it up.

Is there a temperature?

Now you have the location, shape and sensation of the condition, does it move?

Are you willing to let this condition go?

I want you to go inside your body and take it out. You can read that sentence again. Just imagine you're reaching inside your body and taking the 'thing' out.

With your eyes still closed, imagine it in your hand. See the colour, the shape. Is it hard or can you mould it? Roll it up into a ball, go on, play with your condition. Toss it up into the air a few times and when you're ready, throw it away, saying 'goodbye' to it, or 'this no longer bothers me'. To your surprise you can get rid of it.

Now look inside. Are the symptoms still there? The same or changed? Let's focus on it a while longer.

How big is it now? What colour? Shape? Reach in and take it out of your body. How does that feel?

Hold it in your hand. Can you bend it? Drop it on the floor. Does it make a sound? Does it smash into pieces? Pick it up and roll it into a ball again. Tell yourself you no longer want it and hurl it away.

Is the condition still there? Know that you can do the process again. As you reduce the condition, mentally you get stronger and heal yourself.

Gently get centred back into your body and open your eyes.

You can also use that exercise on emotional issues of anger, grief or fear.

I'd like to introduce noesitherapy – healing by thinking – and here credit the founder, Dr Angel Escudero, a surgeon in Valencia, Spain. It has been investigated by many medical experts who have praised his method, he has lectured to the medical world and he has been featured on a number of TV broadcasts around the globe. Dr Jonathan Royle, who taught me this, uses noesitherapy as part of his 'complete mind therapy'.

The theory behind noesitherapy stems from the fight or flight response which we inherited from our caveman ancestors. It is basically the way adrenaline flows through your body. When this happens your muscles are strengthened, which means you can fight more vigorously or run away more quickly. Our caveman was constantly on full alert, especially out hunting. He would fight (anger) an opponent or an animal, but there would still be fear, so his mouth would go dry, muscles would tense and he would have extra strength due to the physiology of the body. When he defeated his foe or killed the animal, he would sigh with relief.

If he met an animal that wanted him for its dinner, then flight (anxiety) would be his action. If he managed to get away, he sighed with relief and – take note – again his mouth was dry. That's the key. After any stress is over, saliva returns to the dry mouth. We also sigh and the muscles relax. I'll not get involved here with the other physical signs of heartbeat, sweating, blood pressure, digestion, which through thousands of years of conditioning is in us humans who now live in a different age. Just remember the saliva.

It's the apprehension, fear or expectancy of feeling pain that makes pain hurt or exist at all. You finish a DIY task and go to the sink to wash your hands and see blood. No sensation occurred when the cut happened as your mind was somewhere else. The moment you see the blood, the cut starts stinging and funnily enough, bleeds more.

If you're injured and are told you have to live with a certain amount of pain, then being able to reframe your mind so there's no pain, maybe just a little discomfort, makes it bearable.

Use the zero to ten scale to judge how much pain you're experiencing.

Besides breathing deeply, your body is conditioned to relax with saliva. Use the idea of a lemon to get saliva working in your mouth. Let's suppose your right elbow is injured. Imagine you're eating a tangy, juicy lemon, get the saliva on your tongue. This part is going to sound daft. Say to yourself, aloud if you can, while the saliva is on your tongue, 'My right elbow is now completely anaesthetised.' Say it three times.

The concept is that the first time the subconscious may ignore the conscious command as it's busy with other tasks. Ask a second time, the subconscious realises you are there and kicks in; the third time the subconscious knows it's true and activates in a way that's right for you. Dr Escudero does it with his patients and he then carries out amputations.

Take a nice, deep, relaxing breath. Imagine your right elbow has gone cold, it's like a lump of meat from a freezer. No discomfort to concern you. In a moment you can swallow the saliva, just say a few affirmations to yourself such as you feel no discomfort, you can turn off pain like a switch. Where is the pain now on the zero to ten scale?

There have been lots of studies and much research carried out using hypnosis for pain relief. There are many practical reasons why hypnosis can help if you are suffering through pain or injury, relief from it being a major factor. Another advantage is the avoidance of any side affects following the use of chemical anaesthetic or medication.

One of the easiest is called glove anaesthesia. Find a comfortable place where you know you will not be disturbed, close your eyes and relax. Think about your breathing, let it be steady, deep and slow. Imagine all the muscles in your body relaxing one by one, from the top of your head, down slowly to the tips of your toes. Focus on each of the muscles of your body as you imagine them melting, softening, and feel at peace in your mind.

Use your imagination to take yourself to a favourite place, somewhere you can feel relaxed and safe. Imagine the sights of that place, any sounds, feel any good feelings you would feel.

Remind yourself you have the power and ability to control any sensations in your body, because you do! Tell yourself you are in control of your mind. You have unlimited power in your mind and you can create numbing sensations in any part of your body.

Develop belief in yourself and the power of your mind grows stronger – go on, encourage and empower yourself. Imagine the words that you say to yourself are being delivered to the deepest depths of your being and are being accepted on every level of your body and mind.

Concentrate now upon your dominant hand, really focus on it now and notice the smallest sensations within it. Using your imagination notice your dominant hand is free of all feeling. Imagine it is encased in ice. Really imagine how that would feel.

Tell yourself your hand is becoming numb, no feeling at all. Tell your mind your hand has gone to sleep. Be aware of all the unusual sensations as you concentrate on it. Tell yourself every breath you take causes your hand to become colder, number, until you just cannot feel your hand at all. You just cannot feel it, no feeling, completely numb.

Now you can transfer that lack of feeling to the part of your body that you want to have the anaesthesia. Just raise your numb hand and place it on the part of your body you want to feel numb. Maybe you can imagine the numbness as a colour spreading into that area. Imagine all those sensations of numbness being transferred into the injured part of your body, coldness all over the area. Breathe deeply and relax.

When you are sure you have achieved anaesthesia, say the word 'anaesthesia' to yourself so each time you use the word in the future, it will help bring in the resources of numbness. Believe each time you choose to use this routine in the future, it will enhance and amplify your control over your body.

Give yourself a time limit this is going to last for. You do not want that body part to be numb for a lifetime. Make sure you set yourself a time limit when your anaesthesia will end.

If you feel pain or undue stiffness, get it looked at. No matter how confident you are, injuries do plant doubts in your mind, which is why the mental side of recovery is so important. Now, it's important for me to make this next distinction for you clearly – you are not injured anymore! You are in a state of recuperation!

Depression can be dealt with…

DEPRESSION

Meet it and you do not see its face. Follow it and you do not see its back.

Lao Tzu

This is serious as we are beginning to hear more about depression within cricket circles. Is it an excuse to cop out, or something more? Actually it's more than feeling low, and when it affects someone it can be a serious illness. Getting through the day can be difficult and through life may seem impossible. This is why people with depression find it difficult to function each day as it affects their physical and mental health and robs them of the ability to think rationally. A cycle of depression can occur after a setback drags on and then other things happen which multiply the situation and the problem seems far worse.

Depression is more common than you might think. It's also indiscriminate. No matter how rich, clever or talented someone is, something like one in five females and one in eight males in the western world will experience some form of depression in their lifetime. It may be only mild, but depression left undiagnosed and untreated can take people onto a more serious level.

145

Cricket is not immune and we have seen a number of cricketers affected by it in different ways over the years. A small but significant number have taken their own lives through not being able to cope. Does the nature of cricket lead to frustration and disappointment? According to David Frith in his book *Silence of the Heart, Cricket Suicides* professional cricketers statistically are more likely to take their own life than any other group of men in the west.

As you may have read earlier in this manual, negative thinking affects feelings and therefore emotions. In sport psychology speak, depression is linked to burn-out, mental exhaustion and unexplained underperformance syndrome – however they are all the same illness.

Knowledge is the first step in helping team-mates who are suffering. 'Pull yourself together' just will not work, neither is it advisable to sit back and say nothing if you know someone who is stumbling through. Look out for your team-mates and assist where you can.

Everyone goes through hard times at some point in their career, so it is important to have good friends and colleagues to help through the personal struggles of fitness, injury, form, family or work. At times like these it can be hard to know what to do, how to help your friend, or you can find it hard to ask for help if it affects you.

Diagnosis must be left to medical experts, but to understand something about depression it is important to understand how people can suffer from it. There are several features that can cause a cricketer to be depressed. Research has shown that depression can run in families for generations. Trauma and stress from financial problems, relationship breakdowns, family bereavement, can all bring on depression.

Injury and illness can contribute to depression, partly because of the physical weakness and stress they bring on, while depression can make medical conditions worse as it weakens the immune system . Some medications can cause depression.

Depression may be caused by chemical imbalances in the brain, but these are due to the emotions being felt, or more likely, emotions not being felt and expressed, but being suppressed and bottled in. As the subconscious harbours negative and unhappy thoughts, the chemicals which make us feel good decrease.

Those good-feel chemicals are serotonin, dopamine and intrinsic endorphins. Serotonin manages contentment and plays a role in our quantity of appetite, aggression, anger, mood and sleep. Dopamine is associated with the feelings we get from reward after achieving a goal. People who lack dopamine are unmotivated and depressed. Endorphins are produced during strenuous exercise, excitement and sex and help us decide whether an experience is pleasurable or painful.

People become slaves to their minds and their emotions. Strong and traumatic events create turmoil in their lives. Anger turned inwards, unexpressed trapped emotions, repressed negative feelings, psychosomatic illness, all cause feelings leading to phobia, panic attacks, extreme stress and depression.

There are numerous forms of depression. Slightly different symptoms may require different treatments. Briefly a major depression, also known as clinical depression, is classed as a depressed mood that lasts for at least two weeks. Psychotic depression is a depressed mood when the sufferers hallucinate, they see and hear things that are not there. There is also paranoia where they feel everyone is against them. Dysthymia is a less severe depressed mood which can last for years. There is mixed depression and anxiety which shows a combination of symptoms, and bipolar disorder, formerly known as manic depressive disorder, which involves periods of feeling down reversed by feeling high.

How do you know if a person is depressed or just going through a bad time? There are some indications when sadness could progress to depression. Someone could be depressed if for more than two weeks they have been down, miserable or sad a majority of the time, or they have lost interest or enjoyment in most of their usual activities and experienced the warning signs in at least three of the following four categories:

1. *Behaviour. They have stopped going out, they are not getting things done, turning to alcohol and sedatives, unable to concentrate and withdrawing from family and friends.*

2. *Feelings. Disappointment, frustration, guilt, indecision, irritability, lack of confidence, feeling miserable, over-whelmed, unhappy.*

3. *Physical. Churning stomach, headaches, loss of appetite, muscular pains, run down, sleep problems, tiredness, weight loss or gain.*

4. *Irrational thoughts. 'I'm a failure', 'It's my fault', 'I'm worthless', 'My life's bad'.*

It's not always easy to help a team-mate because you may not know what to do or say for the best. Maybe they say they don't want any help. They have to accept that they have a problem before it can be resolved. Denial can make it difficult for someone to take the first step in seeking help. It's important to stick with your team-mates when times are rough for them, even if it's just to listen. They need support from friends and family as well as treatment by doctors and psychologists.

To help someone, show interest in them. Encourage them to explain what they are thinking and feeling. Listen without interrupting. Don't show shock on your face. Don't make light of what they are saying. Don't look for quick-fix solutions. Sympathise. Ask them what they want to do about the problem.

Don't place more pressure on your mate by telling them to 'snap out of it'. Don't avoid them. Don't pressure them to party more. Alcohol and substance abuse often appear alongside depression. Discourage your team-mate or friend from using them. Eating disorders and anxiety also appear with depression.

Antidepressants from the doctor don't always help as it can become difficult to come off certain types due to withdrawal symptoms, including anxiety. Correct counselling, along with meditation, enables the sufferer to adjust and change for the better. Cognitive behavioural therapy (CBT) has been recommended to combat mild to moderate depression as it breaks habitual negative thinking. Just talking to a counsellor can be a blessing. The counsellor may ask the sufferer to keep a diary and write down whenever they feel angry, anxious, guilty or upset in any way and describe what the feelings would achieve. This can challenge negative thoughts by considering positive alternatives.

Previous sufferers of clinical depression who have come off prescription drug addiction demonstrate a glimmer of hope with the mantra 'meditation not medication', relegating the grim period of their lives into the past. For some, medication can be the answer while others will respond better to CBT.

Help your team-mate get information, perhaps from a library, health centre or website. Help them make an appointment and go along with them if that is their wish. Have them remember past achievements and successes. Use guided visualisation with an outcome toward positive results; you learned visualisation earlier, didn't you! Encourage the person to get further involved in the club's social activities, fundraising or coaching juniors if appropriate.

Supporting someone who needs it can sometimes be difficult and emotionally draining, especially over an extended period. You don't have to go through it on your own. Find your own team-mates, colleagues or counsellors to talk to. Make sure you continue to enjoy your cricket and other activities, take time out to have some fun and keep things in perspective.

Next – do you have a ritual or superstition…?

SUPERSTITIONS

Captaincy is ninety percent luck and ten percent skill. But don't try it without that ten percent.

Richie Benaud

The world of cricket is made up of numerous influences and variables: equipment, tactics, the intricacies from Mother Nature, and the ever-changing game dynamics that we cannot predict or control and which would have some believing that luck and not talent is the main ingredient for success.

Some individuals will use rituals and routines no matter how bizarre to bring order and stability to their world and keep them from harm or accident. Skill and physical condition are often not enough to protect a player from a perceived danger.

With practical wisdom, it can be reassuring as it makes sense to have some order. You may already have a routine for laying out your kit, inspecting your equipment or examining your fixture list. Have you ever thought about your preparations and come across something you normally do, but didn't? The result can sometimes bring negativity and self-doubt before the game begins, followed by fretting, wondering and worry.

You may have a ritual, such as a particular eating habit, or be fussy about a favourite article of clothing you always wear. Perhaps you have a lucky talisman, a horseshoe or a four-leaf clover fixed onto your bat. A cricketer emotionally attaches success or failure to these irrational rituals, hoping they can enter the performance zone prior to competition.

If a particular object is associated with a win, this increases a need in the player for that ritual or object every game. This will increase with intensity the more important the game.

Not all superstitious behaviour is healthy. It is often difficult for someone to recognise that although routines seemed to work in the past, they are no longer useful. Taking superstition to extremes can lead to rigidness and magical beliefs so that some players can get completely distressed if their routine is upset. A player who dons and fastens each piece of clothing and equipment in exactly the same way every time may have to undress and start again if something happens out of sequence. Someone else may ritually burn something after a bad game.

There is no such thing as luck, only the perception of it. The more dedication, preparation, research, training you do consistently and persistently to get you to your reward, the more chance you have of creating your own luck.

The more you practise the luckier you get. Okay, there is an aspect in every game that you cannot control, so for a great performance you need that something extra. That something extra comes from the long, hard training you have spent to develop your skill.

You may know pessimistic players who think once they get into a bad run, it will continue, or having a good run, they expect it to end.

Once you do get into a run of success, there is no logical reason why it cannot continue. You can forecast that you will go into a barren patch sometime, but it does not last when you keep your thinking right. Class is permanent, form is temporary.

Look over your progress with review...

REVIEW

Batting is a trial before an eleven-man jury.

Richie Benaud

As the leaves fall and the temperature drops, the end of the season has arrived. Now is the time to rest, put your equipment into storage and take a well-earned break. Many cricketers will do an end-of-season equipment inventory without realising that it is they who are the most important piece of equipment they have. Before the past campaign becomes a distant memory, realise that there is no off-season. This is the time for review and improvement.

Breaks are welcome and even necessary to avoid burnout, even if you enjoy every minute of cricket. There are a number of plans you can apply to sharpen your skills. Review your season's performance. Did you do well? Or did your performance begin to fall off as the season wore on?

Accurate self-assessment is required to make positive change. Recognise and understand your behaviours, feelings and thoughts. Check your season averages and reflect on your most successful matches, runs scored, wickets taken. Spend some quality time remembering those games; by doing this, you are storing those successful events to recall when needed.

No matter how well the season went, you may be aware of an area or two that need improvement. Learn from any season failures. Pick out a technique or two you need to improve on and make a promise to find practice time to improve. Create a practice plan. Set goals. Your favourite cricketer did not reach the top just by tossing the ball about. The best spend far more time practising than performing.

In any competitive sport, besides our personal lives, we develop dreams, ideas, and make plans. Those good intentions fall by the wayside as they become forgotten and abandoned during the close season. Don't take a shallow approach to improvement, take responsibility to understand the root cause of any problem. It's easy to do the things you do well, but for personal success, spend time improving those weak areas. Correct any mistakes in technique rather than keep doing the same thing and expecting a different result.

There are some players who are extremely self-disciplined. They go to the gym three times a week, practise indoors, visualise. You may know someone like that no matter how rare they are. Forcing yourself to develop more discipline might become an exercise in frustration. You then go through the tedious, lonely, unhappy task of training without team-mate support. It's a struggle and procrastination wins.

One of the hardest things to do in sport is to keep practising with enthusiasm when you are already good at something. If you begin to slacken off it could have consequences. Recognise that in fact some chores are rewarding.

What would you like to do? Watch a test match DVD or oil your bat? Write a list of several topics you could put some effort into, perhaps equipment maintenance, flexibility exercises, catching practice, rule book study. After each subject, notice how much time you could devote to it and how often. Form these questions: What?

When? Where? Why? How? Then put them in order of preference, the most important to you being at the top.

Cut yourself some slack as you cannot do everything and you need this close season for recuperation. But have a little think about any other subjects you could do but are not listed and write down why this would be important.

Mental rehearsal and visualisation will enhance future performance. There has been much psychological research on the value of mentally rehearsing specific techniques, which shows improvements equal to that achieved by individuals who have spent time in physical practice.

Perform the mechanics of bowling correctly a few times. Next, put the ball down and spend five minutes with your eyes closed, visually repeating what you just did. See if you can create in your mind each particular movement. Notice the position of your fingers and thumb on the ball, feel the stitching, sense yourself going through the arm movement, the release as the ball heads toward its target. You may be able to recreate the physical sensations in your hand and arm as you made the perfect delivery.

Now replay that picture again and see if you can be even more detailed. Do it four or five times more, then pick up the ball and carry out more physical practice. Over time, the combination of physical and mental rehearsal will improve your technique more than either method alone.

Review any mistakes you made last season and replay them in your mind, visualising what you would do differently now. Once you have a picture and feeling of correcting that outcome, replay it over and over again so you can rewrite your own personal history.

Visualise a picture in your mind of yourself holding a trophy at the end of next season.

In learning skills, ask the question 'how'? Improvement and fitness come in gradual peaks, then they plateau and nothing seems to move forward despite your diligent practice. However, realising that, followed by continued practice, will eventually give you a burst of improvement, so keep at it. Remember how far you have come.

I'm sure you will pay attention to your fitness. Develop better endurance, mobility, flexibility and strength. Do you know any sportsperson who was a worse player for being fitter? Do regular exercise so it's not such a big deal getting into shape for the start of the new season. And watch your weight.

Be persistent in your goal for cricket success. Even during the playing season, do something to review your progress, maybe on the first of the month, or the fifteenth.

Match up with team-mates and create a positive environment for the off-season. This will make it more likely you will make improvement and develop the habits you need to become a more consistent cricketer. You can rely on each other for ideas, honest feedback, encouragement and social support.

Share this book and discuss the ideas; some are radical enough to create debate, become inspired and make you think more.

You can stay motivated with a cricket scrap book…

CRICKET SCRAP BOOK

Peak performers from various fields maintain their childlike qualities!

Lars Eric Unestahl

Anyone wanting to invest time in cricket is advised to learn as much as they can about the sport. Read match reports, books, magazines, and watch films. Take clippings or photocopies of pictures, diagrams and photos. Collect brochures of anything to bring into your cricketer's life.

Every time you look at them, it reminds you of the goals yet to be achieved, your role models, places you would like to play, equipment you would like to own. It keeps an account of your cricket activities, training logs, events, symbols, anything that gives you motivation and support.

Use cricket bookmarks. Drink from a cricket mug. Dream in cricket bedding.

How about a video/DVD scrapbook? Watch the top players, study what works for them. Pay close attention and watch everything you can about what s/he does. Psychology, research and real-life experience all prove to us that watching talented cricketers is a great way to learn.

Your successful performance depends on your awareness toward improvement, perception, observation and then feedback.

Here's a way to analyse yourself. You may have to borrow, rent or purchase a video camera. Talk somebody into spending an hour or two helping you. Get a tripod, manually focus on where you stand and film yourself.

When you go home, review the film. You may be surprised. I guarantee as you watch yourself you will notice things about your technique that you did not realise you were doing and you may be able to uncover information about what's clearly been a 'blind spot' in your form.

Keep larger items about your home or room that act as powerful anchors. Look at and handle them frequently. Use regular rehearsal time to smell the leather and feel the texture of the ball, swing the bat. Give yourself a sensory-rich experience. Concentration and rehearsal bring in countless nerve impulses.

Going slightly further, it may be helpful to concentrate on an object, a bat, ball, glove, even a poster on your wall. Study it while being relaxed. Use the exercise like a meditation session. When you notice your thoughts begin to wander, return your full attention to your object. This exercise will improve your ability to focus and give you awareness of where your mind goes.

Get a picture of your hero in action, an exceptional wicket keeper, a batsman of high quality owning a large range of strokes.

Splice a photo of your head onto their body. Put it somewhere you can view it often. You may not possess all your hero's qualities, but you're empowering your mind and stretching it beyond any limitations. Read the 'Mirroring' chapter again, then copy and pretend until you become your own hero. Learn from the legends.

Learn by daydreams…

DAYDREAM

Yes, Arjan, I dream. For only those who can dream can make their dreams come true.

Bhuvan Laagan

As you enter the playing arena a sea of colour greets your eyes and you hear the crowd roar. You look to one side and you feel the energy from your supporters as they sway and swing in jubilation. With pride you notice that every cell of your body feels as if it is tingling with excitement. Smelling the freshly cut grass your excitement mounts as you hear the announcer call out your name, you see your name on the waving, silken banners. Your name.

One of our luxurious pleasures is daydreaming. You see yourself as the James Bond of the cricket world, you bowl faster than a launched missile, your fielding is more agile than a speeding cheetah. You arrive to bat in the nick of time to save the game, or, injured and limping, your bowling wins the cup in the last few balls, the stumps falling like skittles.

It does not stop as you get older. Your dreams may become more modest and limited. Now you join a failed team as a no-nonsense coach, introducing revolutionary techniques, you right all wrongs and reconquer the world.

Would you call it all wishful thinking? I would say it was all subconscious rehearsal. Daydreaming, visualisation, imagination, call it what you want, but when you engage in it, you bring in all the relevant sights, sounds, feelings, smells and if appropriate, tastes. So make your daydream full of life's rich juices.

Make your daydreams of cricket success more fun. When you daydream you are also learning and as you may understand from earlier chapters, you're not doing it in real time. A one-day match could take ten minutes in your mind and as you can contract or expand time, you are in control. Knowing that, you can use your conscious mind to direct your subconscious.

Using any form of mental imagery provides a positive emotional training aid which can help you achieve positive results because they communicate to your nervous system very clearly your desire to see yourself excelling. By daydreaming, you have the opportunity to get things right, so reinforcing to your subconscious the habit of winning.

End of play is upon us…

CONCLUSION

Sports Psychology is the least studied of all cricket skills,
even if it is widely accepted as being the most important
ingredient of success.

Justin Langer

I'm out! There's not been a lot published on the psychological demands of cricket. I hope I have started a new trend. Being physically fit and technically adept is only part of being prepared these days. Mental and emotional strength are also required. I've covered mind techniques that can change your cricket, not just now, but progressively for years to come. This was written with cricketers in mind, however many of the methods described are able to cross over into other areas of your life. As you become familiar with them, your energy and motivation will improve.

If you do nothing, what will happen? If you do something, what will happen? Being in sport you should realise the importance of practice, practice, practice!

Even a small change to your thinking can make a big difference. As you continue with the new way, you'll begin to realise how much you've changed. Don't look how far you have to go, rather how far you have come. As you have learnt, the conscious mind can only think of one thing at a time – why not make it something positive? You can, can you not?

You're often the last person to notice any changes. Keep an ear open for comments from friends or cricket colleagues. Maybe they will comment on how happy you have been lately, how your delivery is improving or how you're becoming a more confident all-rounder.

You should make this book important enough to return to it several times to get the results you need. Why not carry it around in your kit bag? No single technique is a magic pill, but when you practise them repeatedly, they will become familiar. You can even go to the beginning and start reading again.

When I was learning to drive I practised again and again until I was confident enough to pass my test, just as drivers before me had done. All I needed was the confidence practice would bring. I didn't presume driving would not work on my first attempt. Please keep that in mind. If a mind method does not work on your first attempt, don't give up on it. Understand that these tried and tested techniques do work. They work beautifully. You may even find one an exciting and rewarding activity.

Imagine staring into a mirror after a match and honestly telling the person you see there, 'You've done your best.' Feeling the pride and joy of a perfect performance. The delight you have created for your team-mates, the fans, the directors, your coach and your mind coach – sorry about that blatant 'sales plug'.

I sincerely hope you enjoy what's presented here and I really want you to succeed, because by your success this manual will be judged. Have fun and enjoy your cricket.

Some suggestions have been indirect, embedded into the wording of the text to place them into your subconscious mind.

The time to start using them is now…

BIBLIOGRAPHY

Al Huang, Chungliang and Lynch, Jerry. *Thinking Body, Dancing Mind.* Bantam Dell Pub Group (Trd) (Sept 1992). ISBN: 978-0553089622.

Andrew, Keith. *The Skills of Cricket.* The Crowood Press Ltd; New edition (April 1986). ISBN: 978-0946284931

Bolstad, Dr Richard. *Resolve.* Crown House Publishing (March 2002). ISBN: 978-1899836840.

Callahan, Dr Roger and Trubo, Richard. *Tapping the Healer Within.* McGraw-Hill Contemporary; New edition (Jun 2002). ISBN: 978-0809298808.

Complete Editions. *Cricket Sayings.* Complete Editions (2005). ASIN: B000SDT4Q0.

Court, Martyn. *The Winning Mindset.* Trafford Publishing (April 2005). ISBN: 978-1412029667.

Eason, Adam. *The Secrets of Self-Hypnosis.* Network 3000 Publishing (July 2005). ISBN: 978-0970932198.

Edgette, John H & Rowan, Tim. *Winning the Mind Game.* Crown House Publishing (July 2003). ISBN: 978-1904424024.

Francis, Tony. *The Zen of Cricket*. Hutchinson; 1st edition (June 1992). ISBN: 978-0091746483.

Hanin, Y. L. *Emotions in Sport*. Human Kinetics (Nov 1999). ISBN: 978-0880118798.

Hodgson, David. *The Buzz*. Crown House Publishing; illustrated edition (Nov 2006). ISBN: 978-1904424819.

Hughes, Simon. *Jargonbusting: Mastering the Art of Cricket*. Channel 4 Books; New edition (May 2002). ISBN: 978-0752265087.

Lazarus, Jeremy. *Ahead of the Game.* Ecademy Press (Nov 2006). ISBN: 978-1905823093.

Liggett, Donald R. *Sports Hypnosis.* Human Kinetics; 3rd edition (Feb 2000). ISBN: 978-0736002141.

Mack, Garry and Casstevens, David. *Mind Gym*. McGraw-Hill Professional (July 2002). ISBN: 978-0071395977.

McKenna, Paul. *Change Your Life in Seven Days.* Bantam Press; (Jan 2004). ISBN: 9780593066614.

Mycoe, Stephen. *Unlimited Sports Success*. iUniverse.com (June 2001). ISBN: 978-0595186105.

Orlick, Terry PhD. *In Pursuit of Excellence*. Human Kinetics; 3rd Revised edition (Jun 2000). ISBN: 978-0736031868.

Oswald, Yvonne. *Every Word Has Power.* Beyond Words Publishing; 1st Atria Books/Beyond Words Trade pbk edition (May 2008). ISBN: 978-1582701813.

Robbins, Anthony. *Awaken the Giant Within.* Pocket Books; New edition (Jan 2001). ISBN: 978-0743409384.

Robbins Blair, Forbes. *Instant Self-Hypnosis.* Sourcebooks, Inc (April 2003). ISBN: 978-1402202698.

Royle, Dr Jonathan. *Confessions of a Hypnotist.* Exposure Publishing; New edition (Jan 2006). ISBN: 978-1846850523.

Waterfield, Robin. *Hidden Depths.* Pan Books; III Edition (7 May 2004). ISBN: 978-0330492515.

DISCLAIMER

Neither Paul Maher nor Mind Training Arena will be held responsible for any accident or misadventure arising from the improper use of information laid out in this manual. This manual has been written specifically for someone to learn self-hypnosis, not as tuition to hypnotise others.

SELF-HYPNOSIS
FOR CRICKET

Introduction

The use of hypnosis to improve sport performance is well known as a means of enabling a player to live up to their abilities, therefore self-hypnosis is very important.

Let's take it one easy step at a time. To begin, there are many myths about hypnosis, often undeserved, which I should clear up. It's not magical, nor does it give someone magic powers. Nor can it turn you into Superman, otherwise we would all be flying around. You cannot get 'stuck' in hypnosis, you do not put yourself under the power of someone else who will then take control of you. You cannot become possessed. You cannot be made to do something which is against your moral code. You do not leave your body, you do not lose your mind.

Let me reassure you, hypnosis is a natural state of mind which can be used as an efficient psychological tool for a cricketer to reach full potential. Self-hypnosis can be a wonderful vehicle to get you into the performance zone.

Those easiest to hypnotise have the strongest, most creative minds with the greatest ability to use their concentration, imagination and intelligence. Very few people are not able to get into a hypnotic state and there is usually a reason. Epilepsy can create difficulty to focus, and those who are mentally subnormal, have senility or are under alcohol or drug abuse also have difficulty.

Hollywood and the media thrive on drama and many stories in books and on film are the children of fertile imaginations. People lose control at the hands of the evil hypnotist to heighten the tension in the storyline. Those writers themselves have probably been influenced by a previous writer's mistaken idea of what hypnosis is about.

More of the misunderstandings come from stage shows where, I must stress, the participants are in full agreement with the suggestions they have been given. Those people on stage are volunteers who are fully prepared to go along with the entertainment. And that's all it is, entertainment.

With clinical hypnosis, I am not going to get you to bark like a dog, that's not going to cure your bowling problem or help you achieve your innings goal. Hypnosis is a reliable, therapeutic method recognised by orthodox medicine.

Here you will discover how to help yourself achieve success in cricket. Surprisingly you have been in hypnosis many times before, although you may not realise it. A regular journey, to work for example, when you realise you don't remember getting there. Don't worry about anything like that, though, your unconscious is on constant duty, making sure you are safe. As soon as conscious attention is needed, your unconscious gets you there instantly.

How about reading when you realise you haven't noticed a single word because your mind has been some place else? Or you're watching a film and you don't realise someone is talking to you until they start shouting to get your attention, because you have been absorbed by the story on the screen.

These are all forms of hypnosis which happen to you every day. The examples show that you were focused, however, on something else.

Some clients think they failed to 'go under' as nothing more than extreme relaxation took place. They knew they could move or open their eyes if they wanted to, they were just too comfortable to be bothered. That's what hypnosis can be for some people. The best way to describe what you may experience is to remember how you feel just moments before actual sleep occurs, or moments before you wake up. At that moment you pass through a state very similar to hypnosis.

Here are some of the sensations you may experience (it's different for everybody):

- Extremely relaxed

- Floaty

- Tingling in your hands or features

- Feeling either light or heavy

- More awareness, senses heightened

○   Warmth or cold

○   Dry mouth

○   Stress-free

While hypnosis has a great success rate, it does not work for everyone. There is a good chance it will work for you so it's worth giving it a go, isn't it?

Preparation

I'm going to teach you a preparation routine which I would like you to practise. This has been adapted from the self-hypnosis script by Terrence Watts of Hypnosense. Do it with your eyes open a few times so you can read yourself through it, it's easy to remember.

Make sure you won't be disturbed for about ten minutes, and visit the toilet before you begin. Sit comfortably. Some people prefer a straight-backed chair to an armchair. Have both your feet flat on the floor and your hands relaxed in your lap. Notice there is a position where your head feels as if it has no weight. Find that position where your head feels weightless as now it is exactly aligned over your body so your breathing is at its best.

Exercise

Close your eyes, be aware of your breathing and then imagine a feeling of ease and peace drifting down through your body relaxing every muscle. If you find that difficult, imagine how it would feel if your muscles were relaxed. Slow your breathing right down so that you're breathing so gently, you would not disturb a feather placed near your nose.

Don't rush it. Relaxation comes in its own time. After a while, you'll feel yourself bcoming calmer, quieter, your mind as still as your body. It's even fine if you notice that you're more aware than ever before. Stay with it.

And open your eyes when you're ready.

How was that? You can actually go into hypnosis with that simple routine. You may have been surprised at just how easily you can do it!

Visualisation

You should practise and become good at visualisation as it will lead you to success in your aims and goals. Some people think they can't visualise anything as they can't 'see' pictures in their mind's eye. You don't have to see something exactly as if you were looking at a photograph. Try this. Remember a short journey you did today. Something as simple as going from your front door to your living room. Imagine in your mind starting out and finishing it. Whatever it was, that's a visualisation for you.

Effective visualisation practice should use more of your senses than visual imagery. This way your other senses can be strengthened. Imagine what coffee smells like. How about freshly cut grass? Can you hear a whistle or crowd applause? What does your hair feel like? Don't touch it, imagine it. You may be more aware of another sense than vision.

Once you get used to it, you'll soon be able to imagine every smell you can think of, any sound you have ever heard, any texture you have felt. Practise, smell things, feel things, listen to sounds.

Exercise

This time, find somewhere comfortable to sit where you won't be disturbed for twenty minutes or so. Put to one side any problems you are having to deal with, they will still be there when you come back. In fact, after some hypnosis work, you may be able to deal with them more efficiently. One easy trick is to visualise a box or even a kit bag where you can place all your mental and emotional difficulties until you have time to sort them out.

Go through the preparation routine as before and this time, when you are ready, recall some ordinary event that's happened in the last day or so. Remember your senses. How did it look? How did it sound? How did it feel? How did it smell or taste?

With practice, your memories will become more detailed. These images, when used in hypnosis, provide an edge to creating maximum success, as you shall see.

Let's get into self-hypnosis.

Self-Hypnosis

You should now be comfortable with the preparation and visual routines, as I'm going to explain to you a three-part routine for getting into the hypnotic state.

But first, how do you come out of self-hypnosis? Simply finish the session by telling yourself to do so. Tell yourself you will be wide awake and alert, feeling fine on the count of five, then count yourself up from one to five and open your eyes. Practise that a few times.

Part 1

Close your eyes. Bring to mind a special day that you have had, a great day out on a beach during a holiday, a walk in the woods, a time with friends. Notice how the memory starts, remember it and store it in your mind, you will use it later. Bring all your senses in now, remembering what you saw, what you heard, what you felt, even what you smelt and tasted if they are relevant.

Make everything real in your mind and keep focused until you can almost relive one or more of those senses. It will often be the visual one, but don't let it concern you if you don't get it exact, it takes practice. As long as you have an awareness that something is there, that is fine enough. Allow it to happen rather than force it happen.

Part 2

With your eyes closed, imagine you are breathing peace into every cell of your body, each and every fibre of your being. And with every exhalation, you are letting go of any tension. Let each and every muscle from your head down to your toes go limp as you exhale and repeat the word 'peace'. After half a dozen or so breaths, let yourself imagine you are drifting further down and you are becoming more relaxed, more than you have ever been. If you feel yourself floating up, just go with that.

Part 3

Remember in Part 1 storing the memory of a perfect day? You are going to use that now as an anchor for getting into self-hypnosis. This is best achieved after getting some practice with the first two parts. To use this trigger is very simple. After doing the preparation routine (it gets easier and faster the more you practise) and once you become settled using Part 2, bring your happy memory to mind and let it help you drift down into a nice relaxed trance – it's that easy.

When you're ready, count yourself out.

I or You

There are countless ways to achieve self-hypnosis, the method I have shown you is just one. When you're in your trance, read a prepared script or use a tape recorder to give yourself your desires. It's best to work on one thing at a time.

It's usual for people to say 'I will', 'I can', 'I'm going to'. This may be fine for you, but some people respond better by being told what to do, such as 'you will', 'you can', 'you're going to'. It doesn't matter what you use, 'I' or 'you', as long as you use the form that feels right for you. If you're unsure, make a script or recording, using both versions to see which one you better respond to, just don't mix the two up.

Reading a script is as good as making a recording once you get yourself into hypnosis. Have you ever been so absorbed in a book you lost all sense of time? Someone spoke to you and you didn't notice them? That's hypnosis. Once you're in hypnosis just tell yourself you will open your eyes and start reading following Part 3, read, then at the end of the script, close your eyes ready to count yourself up. For either script or recording, you may enjoy some quiet relaxation music playing in the background.

Now I'll show you how to use the state of hypnosis to achieve mastery.

Uses

Let's look at how to actually use self-hypnosis to achieve your goals and desires.

Be sure you're now used to getting into and out of hypnosis; if you're not, your efforts will be wasted. I can't repeat this enough, you must have a full grasp of how to do it. The direct suggestions you will give yourself have to be compounded, so practise until it's so ingrained it will be an automatic response.

You will always be aware of sounds as you're not asleep, so simply relax. So if anything noisy happens outside, you're covered. Any sound you hear will not affect or disturb you, in fact you can actually use any sound to deepen the trance. If there is heavy traffic outside, just tell yourself that all the traffic noise will help you to be more comfortable, more deeply relaxed.

Caution

At the start of the session always tell yourself as a safety device that you will awake immediately if your full attention is needed for any emergency situation. A further caution is not to drive or operate any machinery during your self-hypnosis session as it can slow down reflexes.

You can make yourself feel better, change habits, learn, block pain and so much more. Just decide what goal you need. For setting your goals, there are four 'must' rules which apply to every goal:

Plausible And Realistic

You and I are not magicians. If you are seventy years old you will not play for the Ashes. If it's not possible without hypnosis, it's not possible with it. If you can't vary the flight and pace of your deliveries, then hypnosis won't create mastery instantly for you; however, hypnosis can get you to the highest standard possible for you to produce those deliveries.

Suitable For Personality

For your goal to succeed, it should reflect your personality. Although hypnosis allows people to behave in a way which is different from their 'norm', that's only temporary, so is no good for long-term goals. Select a goal which would not surprise a family member that you were doing it, then use hypnosis to speed up the process and become proficient at it.

Make It Clear

You need to know what it is that you want. Many sportspeople say, 'I want to be a winner.' Okay, a winner at what? Your subconscious has the mind of a seven-year-old, it works only with uncomplicated, simple statements, not ambiguous ones. 'I want to average at least two centuries every season' is a clear goal. That is achievable.

Make It Positive

Think of what you want, not what you don't want. What you can do, not what you can't. What you like, not what you don't like. 'I don't cover my off stump enough' is not a positive statement. 'I want to cover my off stump competently' is. By implication, consciously they mean the same to you, but the literal-minded unconscious does not understand implications. 'I am determined not to be bowled out' is a negative statement. 'I am determined to protect my wickets' carries a different message to your subconscious, which can only function on what IS, not understanding what IS NOT.

The Four Senses Test

You should apply at least four of your senses to your visualisation of any goal. You should SEE yourself doing it successfully, receiving a reward perhaps; HEAR something associated with it, applause maybe; FEEL something associated with it, how about the cool metal of that trophy in your hands; and then SMELL or TASTE something there, celebratory champagne for example.

Now turn all that into a living DVD, make it a rich, sense-filled experience you can go over and over in your mind. As you practise using your senses, you will expand your conscious awareness.

It's best to work on one goal at a time, each goal can run into the next as you progress. Working on one goal at a time makes it more likely that you will achieve it and is a lot easier than trying to remember a jumble of scenarios.

Get yourself into hypnosis and be patient, you cannot hurry it. Once there, play your DVD in your mind three, four, five times and let yourself feel the excitement of this adventure each time. That's an emotional reward for yourself and is an important part of the success plan, so make it your reality.

Each time you do self-hypnosis, you'll do it better than the time before. Want it to happen, let it happen.

You now have the skills to improve your cricket.

Did you enjoy that?

CONCLUSION

That's all there is to it. There is far, far more to the art of self-hypnosis than I have covered here. There are many books, DVDs, courses on this fascinating subject and it's always good to compare more than one person's spin on the subject.

Enjoy your cricket.

For further information visit: www.mindtrainingarena.com